Voices from Around
the World

# VOICES
## FROM AROUND THE WORLD

STECK-VAUGHN
LIBRARY
A Division of Steck-Vaughn Company

*Austin, Texas*

## Program Consultants

Joseph D. Baca, New Mexico State Department of Education

Catharine D. Bell, University of Chicago Laboratory Schools

David L. Depew, Ector County ISD, Odessa, Texas

Miriam M. Glessner, Public Schools, Columbus, Ohio

Gloria P. Hagans, Public Schools, Norfolk, Virginia

Norman McRae, Detroit Public Schools

Anthony L. Rocca, Bellmore, New York

Audrey Tieger, President, California Council for the Social Studies

Theron Trimble, Collier County Public Schools, Naples, Florida

## Acknowledgments

*Executive Editor:* Elizabeth Strauss
*Project Editor:* Anne Souby
*Product Development:* Learning Design Associates, Inc.
*Cover Design:* Joyce Spicer
*Cover Artist:* Susan Melrath

*Title page photo:* Larry Tackett / Tom Stack & Assoc.

*Library of Congress Cataloging-in-Publication Data*
Voices from around the world / written by Steck-Vaughn Company.
p.  cm. — (Voices)
Includes index.
Summary: Real people tell about major world regions with which they are familiar.
ISBN 0-8114-2772-2
1. Geography — Juvenile literature. [1. Geography.] I. Steck-Vaughn Company.
G133.V65   1990
910—dc20        90–10133  CIP  AC

# CONTENTS

# INTRODUCTION

Have you ever thought about what it would be like to live in a totally different place? To spend a winter in Siberia or fish for piranha on the Amazon? To grow up in Egypt in the shadow of the pyramids? Or to be a modern-day rancher in the American West? Where we live plays a large part in determining what life is like for us. This is because landforms, climate, natural resources, plants, and animals differ from region to region. *Voices* shows how Earth's geography helps shape culture and daily life.

Bringing together journal writings, memoirs, and narratives of men and women from many countries, *Voices* provides a fascinating trip around the world, and back in time as well. You'll witness the eruption of a volcano on the coast of Italy, drill for oil in the North Sea, and work in the paddies of a Vietnamese rice farm. You'll read Beryl Markham's moving description of an early flight over the Serengeti Plains of Africa, Admiral Richard Byrd's narrative about his return to Antarctica, and Peter Jacobs's 1852 description of the raw power of Niagara Falls.

The readings in *Voices* take you to all the major regions of the world. Comments introduce each reading to set the scene. Concluding paragraphs provide a follow-up. Maps pinpoint the location of events, and margin notes define unfamiliar words.

The voices in this book tell what life is like in faraway places and close to home. Whether you read these selections to compare life in different places, to gather information, or for rainy-day adventure, you'll discover these voices from around the world speak volumes about the planet we call home.

# CANADA AND THE UNITED STATES

Alaska (U.S.)

Arctic Circle

CANADA

Hudson Bay

0    400    800 MI
0    400    800 KM

PACIFIC OCEAN

UNITED STATES

ATLANTIC OCEAN

N

Hawaii (U.S.)

22°N

0    100 MI
0    100 KM

20°N

20°N

Gulf of Mexico

Tropic of Cancer

If an American were asked to locate the Rocky Mountains, she would probably think of Colorado or Montana. But a Canadian asked the same question might locate them in the Canadian province of Alberta. Who would be right? Both. The Rocky Mountains, one of the highest and most beautiful mountain ranges in the world, stretch from the southwestern United States far across the border into northern Canada. They are a symbol of how naturally Canada and the United States are connected.

Both countries abound with natural resources. Half of Earth's supply of fresh water is found in the lakes of Canada. At least 300 species of fish live in Canada's coastal waters. Together the United States and Canada share the waterways of the Great Lakes. Farmers in the United States grow enough food for the entire country and much of the world.

Both countries are huge. Canada is the second largest country in the world. The United States is the fourth largest. Together, these two giants share the longest undefended border in the world. Towns, farms and ranches, and even homes straddle the line.

What accounts for such peaceful relations between these two giants? It is more than just shared landforms and waterways. Because the two countries have similar histories, they share cultural values and traditions which help to simplify communication and trade between them. Each was colonized by European powers. Each is predominantly Christian. Each is a nation of immigrants.

But such strong physical and cultural similarities can be deceiving. The land and the people may look alike, yet the United States and Canada are distinct and separate countries. The United States fought a war for independence and has long been characterized as an adventurous land of pioneers. The American West was wild and lawless. Canada is one of the few countries to become independent without a revolution. The Royal Canadian Mounties—a symbol of law and order—led the way as Canada expanded west.

The contrasts continue. English is the primary language of the United States, while Canada is a bilingual nation. Both French and English are spoken there. Great Britain gave up all control of the United States in 1783. The British monarch is still the official head of state in Canada.

Currently, the people of the United States and Canada enjoy one of the highest standards of living in the world. This enables the people who live there to maintain a lifestyle they enjoy and attracts many people from other countries. Large numbers of refugees and immigrants are still drawn to these two countries today.

Without a map it would be difficult to tell where western Canada ends and the western U.S. begins. Ranchers on both sides of the border raise cattle on the rolling grasslands.

This unit features Americans and Canadians whose lives have been strongly shaped by the regions in which they live.

- In his diary, Native American Peter Jacobs describes the power and beauty of Niagara Falls and the wilderness surrounding the **Great Lakes** in 1852.
- Gerard Chiasson, a Canadian, explains how he makes his living fishing in **Nova Scotia**.
- Writer Wallace Stegner recalls his childhood growing up along the **United States–Canada border** in the west.
- From **Wyoming**, cattle rancher Helen Musgrave tells writer Teresa Jordan about the issues facing ranchers today.

# Traveling by Canoe

" . . . my whole frame shook as a leaf while I was viewing these mighty angry Falls."

**Peter Jacobs**

In the 1800s artist John Vanderlyn captured the beauty of the Niagara River as it plunged 160 feet over Niagara Falls.

*waterways:* bodies of water that can be used for travel

**D**uring the Ice Age, great glaciers edged across North America, cutting out huge depressions in the landscape. Later, these deep ruts and crevices filled with water to become the Great Lakes and other **waterways.** The Great Lakes are the world's largest group of freshwater lakes. They have been traveled by Native Americans, fur traders, and explorers. Today they provide water routes for shipping products from city to city. Peter Jacobs was an Ojibwa Methodist minister. He describes his travels across the Great Lakes in 1852. ∽

*cataract:* waterfall

*inclining:* tending

*whortleberries:* blue or blackish berries; huckleberries

*portage:* carrying boats and supplies overland to bypass waterfalls or rapids; the overland route used

*On 8 May 1852 Jacobs saw Niagara Falls for the first time.*

. . . I went down to see the greatest fall in the world. The **cataract** is indeed awfully grand; and it appeared to me as if an angry God was dwelling beneath it, for my whole frame shook as a leaf while I was viewing these mighty angry Falls. Now 'tis no wonder that my forefathers, in by-gone days, should offer up sacrifices at the foot of these Falls; they used to come and pray to the God of the fall to bless them in their hunt and to prolong their life and that of their children; for every Indian believed that a God dwelt under this mighty sheet of water. . . .

*On 28 May he saw Kakabeka Falls.*

After an early breakfast, the men began to pole up against a strong current or rapid, somewhere

*discharged:* unloaded

*thirty fathoms:* about 180 feet

about fifteen miles in length. The Banks of the river are high, dry and sandy, the principal timber being birch, poplar, and small stunted pine. The north bank is **inclining** to be like a prairie, where, in the month of July, an abundance of blue berries (**whortleberries**) are to be found. I and eight men got out of the canoes and walked on the north bank of the river for the distance of some miles, and then got into the canoes again. After an hour's paddling, we came to a place where the men were obliged to make a half **portage**, by taking out part of the baggage, the current being too strong, so that when the canoe is thus **discharged** the men pulled them by a cord line about **thirty fathoms** long. After another hour's pull we came to a dead water, that is where the current was strong, and

## Great Lakes Region

apparently no current at all. This was about two miles in length; and at the upper end of this we dined on a fine open space or plain cleared by former fires. After this, I and eight men crossed over to the south side of the river, and followed an Indian trail or path for about three miles, which brought us to the foot of the mountain Portage; and after waiting about fifteen minutes, the canoes arrived. . . . The stone composing this mountain is of the **slate** appearance. The portage itself is about a mile in length. At this place is one of the grandest falls of water to be seen at any of all the many noble rivers of America, and is second in **grandeur** to the greatest of cataracts, that of Niagara. . . .

*He was at Rainy Lake on 25 September.*
. . . It blew very hard, but the wind was in our favor. In two hours we passed the Nahmakaun, or

Sturgeon Lake. When we reached the entrance of the Nahmakaun River, it blew a hurricane; we were glad that we were not **wind-bound**; we congratulated ourselves that we were in a narrow river at this time. We pulled up stream, and made several portages during the day. Nothing worth relating occurred to-day, but I will relate what occurred at the second portage from Nah-makaun in one of my former voy-ages. The fall is four feet high, and is nearly **perpendicular**. The surface of the water where it begins to fall is quite smooth. The fall is so large that voyagers dare not shoot over, as they do in smaller falls. I and my men were coming from Fort William, Lake Superior, with a load of flour, for the use of my family at Fort Frances. I was not able that year to get flour from Red River, on account of the troops being there. We had intended to go near the

*slate:* hard rock that separates easily into thin layers

*grandeur:* splendor; magnificence

*wind-bound:* heading into the wind

*perpendicular:* at right angles. Here, Jacobs means the fall was straight up and down.

5

*pitch:* rough area

*ungovernable:* out of control

*steersman:* person who sits at the back of the boat and steers

*Providence:* God

*eddy:* small whirlpool

*perceivable:* noticeable

**pitch** of the rapids, in order to save ourselves much labor and trouble, and to make a short portage of thirty feet. But in approaching the desired place just above the pitch, we accidentally touched a stone under our canoe, which was immediately whirled round; as there was a strong current besides, the canoe became **ungovernable**. I was **steersman** at the time. The canoe was fast going down on her broadside; our only alternative, therefore, was to go down the falls. It was too late to go back. Down we went. As we were going down, I cried out to my men, telling them to squat at the bottom of the canoe, while I did the same at the same moment. Plash we went; every one of us, without knowing it at the time, lost his paddle. By this time our canoe was half full of water. For a few minutes we were senseless. There was our luggage floating about, the flour-bags were quite wet. My men, as I said before, lost all their paddles, and as I also lost my steering paddle, our canoe was now at the mercy of the rocks below, to be dashed to pieces on striking them.

At this critical moment kind **Providence** sent up my paddle to my hand, that is, by the motion of the water about a whirlpool, my paddle was forced up erect near me, and I laid hold of it, and steered the canoe, so that we evaded the projecting rocks that threatened to break our canoe to pieces, and went to an **eddy**, where my men luckily got their paddles. We soon went down all right again, as if nothing had happened. . . .

*September 27.*

Early this morning we started, and made two portages and two lakes. We had our breakfast at Ogoncekahning Lake. After breakfast the clouds began to gather, and looked as if it was going to rain or snow. At twelve o'clock the snow fell fast and thick; soon it was **perceivable** lying on the ground. At two o'clock in the afternoon we arrived at the French portage. . . .

In making this long portage, I never suffered so much in these cold regions for the whole term of twelve years that I was in them, as I did at this time. It snowed very much, and

Early visitors to Niagara Falls explored the huge ice caverns and icicles formed by freezing winter temperatures. This photograph was taken in 1875.

Niagara Falls is on the border of Canada and the United States, between Lake Erie and Lake Ontario. The Canadian side of the falls is called Horseshoe Falls because of its shape.

the wind was strong. We had to follow a narrow path, on each side of which were pine bushes and other evergreens covered with wet snow. It was impossible to walk on without touching these; consequently our clothes were quite wet from the snow melting on them. We were **drenched** to the skin, and felt very cold by the time we reached the other end of the portage. My men nearly cried from the cold. I was not in a much better state. . . . O how glad we were when we **kindled** a large blazing fire, and **partook** of a hearty supper.

*drenched:* wet; soaked

*kindled:* started

*partook:* ate together

The Great Lakes have long attracted visitors in search of adventure and beauty. Millions of people come to the lakes to climb, camp, and fish. However, many factories are located around the Great Lakes. Water pollution has become a problem. Fish are dying of cancer and other diseases. The United States and Canada have joined forces to clean up the Great Lakes. Both countries are placing more controls on the waste dumped into the lakes.

From *First People, First Voices*, ed. Penny Petrone (Toronto: University of Toronto Press, 1983), pp. 97–99.

# Fishing in Nova Scotia

" . . . we had good fishing for ten days—
but it was murder on the arms."

**Gerard Chiasson**

Gasperaux fishermen in Nova Scotia use nets to retrieve their catch.

*maritime:* relating to the sea

*gaspereaux:* fish related to the herring and shad

*Margaree Forks:* town on Cape Breton Island

*schooner:* ship with two sails

*Margaree Harbour:* town on the coast of Cape Breton Island

*Halifax:* capital of Nova Scotia

*West Indies:* of islands in the Caribbean Sea

*cured:* sufficiently treated to prevent spoiling

*headed:* covered

*brine:* salt water

*rank:* spoiled

*filleting:* removing the bones from

The Canadian province of Nova Scotia is made up of a peninsula of the Canadian mainland and the Atlantic island of Cape Breton. No part of Nova Scotia is more than 35 miles from the Atlantic Ocean. **Maritime** activities, such as shipping and fishing, are the foundation of Nova Scotia's economy. Gerard Chiasson comes from a family of fishers. His father and great-grandfather caught fish for a living. In this reading, he describes his traditional fishing life.

I fished **gaspereaux** with my dad, down at **Margaree Forks**, from the time I was fifteen. We moved up here eleven years ago and I've been fishing fairly steadily since then. . . .

My great-grandfather, Captain Mose, had a **schooner** and he used to haul them from **Margaree Harbour** up to **Halifax** back in 1885—the market of salt fish to the **West Indies** has been going a long time, is still going on.

He prepared them same as we do now. There's no change. They're salted as they come from the river—salted round—100 pounds of salt to 200 pounds of fish. They're allowed to sit in that for fourteen days—then they're **cured**. Then they're re-packed to 200 pounds to each barrel, and they're **headed** with 100 percent **brine**. . . . It's a fish that'll hold well—it can

stand two years in a brine pickle—and it won't get **rank**. . . .

My great-grandfather fished them the same way we do now. Same kind of a trap, on the river. But in the late 1800s, early 1900s, each trap would only get fifteen to twenty barrels. My dad tells me each fisherman that was going to fish, he would have the lumber on hand in the wintertime and the cooper would come around and would make the barrels right at the man's place. We order the barrels from outside now, made by a factory. I ordered 400 this year. In those days fifteen to twenty. . . . But there was no market for them for lobster bait in those days. And now they're **filleting** gaspereaux to replace some of the shortage of herring. They're filleted at big plants here and they're shipped over to Europe in six-pound blocks, frozen—replacing the herring they're not getting there off the coasts. . . .

In 'seventy-three we lost the trap and we fished off the bank for ten days. High water. Lost everything. The ice only left the lake that year the twentieth of May and the twenty-first we had a heavy rain and the ice leaving the lake and it flooded and just cleaned everything completely, any trap that was on the river. And the fish struck the next day. And we had no alternative but to try and we had good fishing for ten days—but it was murder on the arms. You imagine when you're dipping in a trap and you get down to the end, well your gate is there to hold you. But if there's nothing there and you've got half a crate of fish in your net—that terrific pressure on your arms—you had to have a man—a good man—to catch that net. We got two thousand barrels that year. That was good fishing.

Some gaspereaux are preserved in salt. Others are preserved by hanging them in smokehouses.

Nova Scotia ranks first among the Canadian provinces in the value of fish caught. It has one of the largest fish-processing plants in North America. As this reading illustrates, fishing is a laborious way to earn a living. But for those who value the history and tradition of the region, the work is rewarding. And the trade relations established in the 1800s between Nova Scotia and the West Indies still continue.

From *Down North*, ed. Ronald Capland (Cape Breton, Nova Scotia: Cape Breton's Magazine, 1980), pp. 154, 158, 159, 160. Reprinted by permission.

# The 49th Parallel

" . . . the 49th parallel . . . was the beginning of civilization in what had been a lawless wilderness. "

**Wallace Stegner**

Wildflowers cover the Interior Plains of Canada in spring. These plains extend into the Great Plains of the United States.

*Pulitzer Prize:* annual award given for outstanding achievement in literature, and other fields

*Whitemud:* Canadian river in Alberta

*Empire:* British Empire

*Dominion:* self-governing countries in the British Empire

*Union Jack:* British flag

*Ltd.:* limited

*rounders:* game similar to baseball

*Dominion Day:* Canadian holiday similar to the 4th of July

*Victoria Day:* Queen Victoria's birthday

*shoepacs:* waterproof boots

The 49th parallel marks the boundary between the United States and Canada. This boundary was first established in 1818 by the Americans and the British. It ran from what is now the eastern edge of North Dakota to the Rocky Mountains. In 1846 the boundary was extended to the Pacific Ocean. Wallace Stegner is an American writer and winner of the **Pulitzer Prize.** He describes what it was like to grow up between two countries that are so alike and yet so different.

The 49th parallel ran directly through my childhood, dividing me in two. In winter, in the town on the **Whitemud**, we were almost totally Canadian. The textbooks we used in school were published in Toronto and made by Canadians or Englishmen; the geography we studied was focused on the **Empire** and the **Dominion**. . . .

The songs we sang were "Tipperary" and "We'll Never Let the Old Flag Fall" and "The Maple Leaf Forever" and "God Save the King"; the flag we saluted was the **Union Jack**, the heroes we most revered belonged to the Canadian regiment called the Princess Pats. . . . The businesses whose names we knew and whose products we saw advertised were **Ltd.**, not Inc., the games we played were ice hockey and **rounders**, the movie serials that

drew us to the Pastime Theater on Tuesdays and Saturdays were likely to retail the deeds of Mounted Policemen amid the Yukon snows. Our holidays, apart from Thanksgiving and Christmas, which were international, were **Dominion Day**, **Victoria Day**, the King's birthday. Even the clothes we wore had a provincial flavor, and I never knew till I moved to Montana and was taught by the laughter of Montana kids that turtle-necked sweaters and **shoepacs** were not standard winter costume everywhere.

But if winter and town made Canadians of us, summer and the homestead restored us to something nearly, if not quite, American. We could not be remarkably impressed with the physical differences between Canada and the United States, for our lives slopped over the international boundary every summer day. Our **plowshares** bit into Montana sod every time we made the turn at the south end of the field. . . .

The people we neighbored with were all in Montana, half our disk of earth and half our bowl of sky acknowledged another flag than ours, the circle of darkness after the prairie night came down was half American, and the few lights that assured us we were not alone were all across the Line. The mountains whose peaks drew my wistful eyes on July days were the **Bearpaws**, down below the Milk River. For all my eyes could tell me, no Line existed, for the **obelisk** of black iron that marked our southeastern corner was only a somewhat larger version of the survey stakes . . . that divided our world into uniform squares. It never occurred to us to walk along the border from obelisk to obelisk—an act that might have

given us a notion of the boundary as an endless, very open fence, with posts a mile apart. And if we had walked along it, we would have found only more plains, more **burnouts**, more gopher holes, more cactus, more stinkweed and primroses, more hawk shadows slipping over the scabby flats. . . . The nearest custom house was clear over in **Alberta**, and all the summers we spent on the farm we never saw an officer, Canadian or American. We bought supplies in Harlem or Chinook and got our mail at Hydro, all in Montana. In the fall we hauled our wheat, if we had made any, freely and I suppose illegally across to the Milk River towns and sold it where it was handiest to sell it. Even yet, between Willow Creek and Treelon, a degree and a half of longitude, there is not a single settlement or a custom station.

We ignored the international boundary in ways and to degrees

*plowshares:* part of the plow that cuts through the ground

*Bearpaws:* mountains in Montana

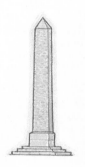

*obelisk:* four-sided pillar that becomes narrower at the top

*burnouts:* land destroyed by fire

*Alberta:* western Canadian province

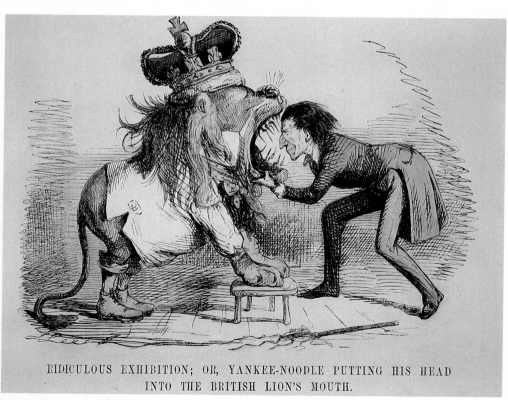

RIDICULOUS EXHIBITION; OR, YANKEE-NOODLE PUTTING HIS HEAD INTO THE BRITISH LION'S MOUTH.

This political cartoon depicts the dispute between Great Britain (the lion) and the United States over control of Oregon, Washington, Idaho, and Montana.

that would have been impossible if it had not been a line almost completely artificial. And yet our summer world was a different world from the Canadian world of town. The magazines to which we now subscribed were American magazines, the newspapers we read were published in **Havre**, **Great Falls**, even Minneapolis. . . . Our summer holidays were the Fourth of July and Labor Day, and the *pièce de résistance* of a holiday get-together was a ballgame. . . .

Undistinguishable and ignored as it was, artificially as it split a country that was **topographically and climatically one**, the international boundary marked a divide in our affiliations, expectations, loyalties. Like the pond at the east end of the Cypress Hills, we could flow into either **watershed**, or into both simultaneously, but we never confused the two. Winter and summer were at odds in us. We were Americans without the education

and **indoctrination** that would have made us confident of our identity, we were Canadians in everything but our sentimental and patriotic commitment. Whatever was being done to us by our exposure to Canadian attitudes, traditions, and prejudices—an exposure intensified by the strains and shortages of **the war** in which Canada was a **belligerent** through four of my six years there—we never thought of ourselves as anything but American. Since we could not explain why the United States was "too cowardly to get into the fight" against Germany, and since we were secretly afraid it was, we sometimes came to blows with the uncomplicatedly Canadian boys. It used to agonize me, wondering whether or not the Canadians really did defeat the Americans at the **Battle of Lundy's Lane** during the War of 1812. It did not seem possible or likely, and yet there it was in the history book. Perhaps I

In this early photo, farm workers gather around a food wagon for lunch. The gently rolling plains and fertile soil made the border area ideal for wheat farming.

reached the beginning of wisdom, of a sort, when I discovered that Lundy's Lane, which loomed like **Waterloo** or **Tours** in the Canadian textbooks and in my anxious imagination, was dismissed as a frontier skirmish by histories written in the United States. The importance of that battle depended entirely on which side of the frontier you viewed it from.

That was the way the 49th parallel, though outwardly ignored, divided us. It exerted uncomprehended pressures upon affiliation and belief, custom and costume. It offered us subtle choices even in language (we **stooked** our wheat; across the Line they shocked it), and it lay among our loyalties as disturbing as a hair in butter. Considering how much I saw of it and how many kinds of influence it brought to bear on me, it might have done me good to learn something of how it came there. I never did until much later, and when I began to look it up I discovered that practically nobody else knew how it had come there either. While I lived on it, I accepted it as I accepted **Orion** in the winter sky. I did not know that this line of iron posts was one outward evidence of the coming of history to the unhistoried Plains. . . . In actual fact, the boundary which **Joseph Kinsey**

Before modern tractors were available, farmers relied on horse power to harvest their wheat.

**Howard** has called artificial and ridiculous was more **potent** in the lives of people like us than the natural divide of the Cypress Hills had ever been upon the tribes it held apart. For the 49th parallel was an agreement, a rule, a limitation, a fiction perhaps but a legal one, acknowledged by both sides; and the coming of law, even such limited law as this, was the beginning of civilization in what had been a lawless wilderness.

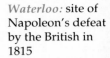

*Waterloo:* site of Napoleon's defeat by the British in 1815

*Tours:* site of a famous battle during the Crusades in 732. The Christians defeated the Muslims.

*stooked:* collected into piles

*Orion:* constellation shaped like a hunter

*Joseph Kinsey Howard:* Montana author (1906–1951)

*potent:* powerful

The United States and Canada share much more than a border. They share many geographic features, such as the Great Lakes and the Rocky Mountains. Most Americans take the similarities in United States and Canadian cultures for granted, but the two countries are also different. Along their peaceful border, the warmest part of Canada meets the coldest part of the United States. Along the border, the two countries look identical. At first, the differences may be hard to see, but to someone who lives on the 49th parallel the differences can be felt instead.

From Wallace Stegner, *Wolf Willow* (New York: Viking Press, 1963), pp. 81–85. Reprinted by permission.

# The American West

Millions of cattle graze on the rolling grasslands that cover much of Wyoming and Montana.

" All this land has to be producing something and can be producing something. "

**Helen Musgrave**

**A** person's relationship to the land depends on many factors. Life on the ranches and farms of rural America brings out a person's respect for the power of nature and our responsibility to the land. Teresa Jordan grew up in Wyoming and understands the connection between people and the land. She covered 60,000 miles interviewing over one hundred rural women about their lives in the American West. She relates the events of the evening she spent with Helen Musgrave, manager of the NX Bar ranch. 

*Teresa:* The average home in the U.S. has what? Fifteen hundred square feet? Add to that the few thousand more square feet that **comprise** your yard and place of business and you have the quarter acre or so in this world that really concerns you. You can enjoy the fiercest thunderstorm from your **window seat**, wrapped in an **afghan** and safe in the knowledge that the chance your tiny space will be hit by lightning is almost **nil**.

But if you were a rancher in **arid** country, where forty acres feeds one cow and your "home" consists of forty thousand acres, your attitude would change. A single bolt can set the prairie ablaze and, fanned by a healthy summer breeze, sweep across the plains, **charring** your summer pasture, licking up your winter haystacks.

Your concern is not only with your own land. Fire pays little mind to fences or **surveyed** boundaries. A neighbor's problem can quickly become your own. In timber country, the trouble doesn't pass with the storm itself. A struck tree can **smolder** for hours, even days, before it flares.

The best you can do is spot a fire when it first breaks out. That's why, among the ranchers in the arid prairie and timber ranchland in northeast Wyoming and southeast Montana, fire-watch is a serious thing. You develop an **acute** sensitivity to sky. The minute clouds start to gather, you, or someone from your ranch, grabs the Jeep and races up the steep **divide**, to sit for hours on a jagged point, watching the storm. . . .

*comprise:* make up

*window seat:* window with a large interior ledge or seat

*afghan:* crocheted or knitted blanket

*nil:* zero

*arid:* very dry

*charring:* burning

*surveyed:* measured

*smolder:* burn slowly with smoke but no flame

*acute:* very keen

*divide:* ridge

**14**

I meet Helen Musgrave, the manager of the NX Bar, in **Sheridan**. . . . We **careen** over the seven miles of rugged dirt road to the NX Bar headquarters and stop there only long enough to grab a couple bedrolls and switch from the car to the **Scout**. Then we bounce over miles of cow tracks and prairie roads, heading up the divide. By the time we reach the top of the **Badger Mountains**, it is nearly dark and the lightning has started in earnest. It is a long way off but nonetheless dramatic. **Vast** walls of sheet lightning turn the evening into day. . . .

We stay on the divide for several hours. Occasionally, on a distant point, we see the lights of a vehicle turn on, drive a short ways, snap off. Another rancher watching the storm. No fires will start this night, but a tree will be struck on a neighboring ranch and smolder for two days before bursting into flame. The whole neighborhood will respond, but several thousand acres will burn before the fire is brought under control. For now, under explosive skies and over the constant rumble and crack of thunder, Helen and I are free to talk. . . .

*Helen:* We're in an energy crisis and we think it's in terms of fuel, but it's also in terms of what we're eating. Calories, nutritious calories, are energy too. I think this point has not been universally recognized in the livestock industry yet. Everybody is thinking about how they're going to manufacture cheaper fuels for tractors and how they're going to get back and forth to town on a cheaper basis. But it goes a lot further than that. When we talk about energy conservation, we shouldn't think only of **fossil fuels**. We should also think about food.

The American consumer is so **outrageously** spoiled and unrealistic in the consumption of food. I include myself in this and everybody around me. We demand the most **elaborate** and expensive packaging techniques. We require fantastic decoration in food **outlets**. The nicer the store, the more **apt** we are to shop there. We're **utilizing** food products that have no real bearing on nutrition and what it takes to survive. . . .

Here we are one of the most **literate** populations in the world, and we don't understand anything

*Sheridan:* Wyoming town

*careen:* lurch from side to side

*Scout:* jeep

*Badger Mountains:* Wyoming mountain range

*vast:* huge

*fossil fuels:* such as oil and coal, formed from the decaying bodies of ancient life forms

*outrageously:* extremely to the point of being ridiculous

*elaborate:* complicated

*outlets:* stores

*apt:* likely

*utilizing:* using

*literate:* educated

Prairie fires caused by lightning can destroy pasture land and livestock. Some ranchers start fires on purpose to burn off the woody plants that can overrun the prairie.

Ranch workers on horseback tend their large herds. Each ranch uses a special brand to identify its cattle.

*verge:* edge

*ironically:* opposite of what one might expect. Musgrave means it is ironic that eating more cheaply will force us to eat better.

*orient:* adjust or adapt

*supplementary feed:* food in addition to grass

*opportune:* convenient or profitable

*under fire:* criticized

*unarable land:* land that cannot be used for farming

*forage:* search for food

*herbivorous:* plant eating

*thrashing:* harvesting

*combining:* harvesting with a combine machine

about nutrition or the production of food or what it means. . . .

We're on the **verge** of big changes. When it becomes cheaper to cook food at home, we won't go out and buy it in a fast-food chain. Not only cheaper, but so much cheaper that it becomes a necessity. **Ironically**, it's then that we'll start eating better. I think at the same time, the food production industry has to **orient** itself towards producing better, more efficient food. For instance, we people who are in the production of livestock, of food off grass, have to be looking for ways to produce something that is nutritionally as good or better for the consumer yet cheaper to produce. We need to look for the animals that will most efficiently turn grass into meat with little or no **supplementary feed**.

I think we have the responsibility as food producers to educate the public. Not towards what we would necessarily want them to buy or what seems most **opportune** for us

to sell, but what is better for us to produce in terms of protein and nutritional efficiency.

Meat has been **under fire** as an inefficient use of agricultural land for a number of years. It's fine to say that meat is not as efficient as grain to produce protein for human consumption, except that we're dealing with land that you can't put into grain production efficiently. Half of the land in the United States is of range character, and something like two thirds of the whole world in **unarable land**. Its greatest production is not in what is actually produced out of the soil. Rather, it's in what eats what is being produced out of the soil. Food chains. You can't efficiently harvest grass or browse or **forage** for human consumption. It's too expensive. If you could do it at all, the amount of feed that you could harvest off this very rough terrain would never pay. So you have an animal, a **herbivorous** animal, that is **thrashing** or **combining** it for you and producing another food product. All this land has to be producing something and can be producing something. It's just a matter of finding out what it produces best in terms of energy.

Nutritional efficiency may **entail** a change in values, like what has taken place in the cars we drive. We're trying now to use cars that don't pollute the environment . . . even though they may not be quite as comfortable to drive. Well, I think food production needs to undergo the same change. We need to rely on food with good nutritional value instead of expensive, empty calories.

In meat production, for instance, fat tissue is going to go out the window. We're producing huge amounts of fat tissue in our domestic cattle and pigs that have no meaning in terms of nutrition to the consumer. It's being produced because it makes the meat tasty and easy to handle. We'll be relying much more heavily on grass-fed meat. And we'll be looking for animals that make the most meat out of the forage they consume.

*entail:*
include; require

Some ranchers raise buffalo instead of cattle. Buffalo are cheaper to feed than cattle and their meat is leaner than beef.

Helen Musgrave has taken an active role in learning to use the land more efficiently. The NX Bar ranch is involved in a wildlife-breeding program. Musgrave raises elk, buffalo, yaks, goats, and many types of cattle. She is looking for the animal that can best use the grass that grows on the Western plains.

From Teresa Jordan, *Cowgirls: Women of the American West* (New York: Anchor Press, 1982), pp. 107–9, 112–13. Reprinted by permission.

# LATIN AMERICA

*Incas:* people who built an empire along the western coast of South America, which lasted until 1532

*Aztecs:* people who built an empire in Mexico. The Aztecs were conquered by the Spanish in 1521.

*Mayas:* people who built a complex civilization in Central America that flourished until A.D. 900

*rain forest:* dense woodland that receives much rain

Picture lofty snow-smothered mountains and rain-starved flatlands, crumbling ruins of ancient pyramids and sleek modern office buildings, flaming red coffee beans and bright green parrots. Add to that picture black faces, brown faces, white faces—Native Americans, Europeans, Africans, Asians. This is Latin America, once the home of mighty Native American empires, then the conquered land of Spanish and Portuguese outsiders. Today Latin America is a "melting pot" in which more than half of the people are of mixed heritage.

Long before Christopher Columbus sailed the seas, the great ancient civilizations of the Western Hemisphere—the **Incas**, the **Aztecs**, and the **Mayas**—were flourishing in the farmable river valleys of Latin America. Some of these valleys were quite high, with tall mountains close by. In these places the climate was less hot, and the soil was best for planting. The Inca settled in the central Andes, hemmed by peaks that soar up to 22,000 feet. The longest continuous mountain chain in the world, the Andes form the backbone of the South American continent.

Out of the Andes flows the mighty Amazon. Latin America has many other rivers, but none compares with this one. The "River Sea," as the people call it, is the longest river in the Western Hemisphere. It carries more water than any other river in the world. Like a wide brown snake, it slithers across 4,000 miles of the South American continent to the Atlantic Ocean. Surrounding its path is the lush, green **rain forest**,

18

alive with the calls of wild birds, monkeys, and frogs. In these hot and steamy woods are more kinds of trees and species of animals than anywhere else in the world.

The hot tropical sun beats down not only on the rain forests but on the plains as well. It scorches the dry salt basins of the Atacama Desert of Chile, one of the the driest areas of the world. It warms the fertile plains—the *llanos* of Colombia and Venezuela, where cattle have grazed since the 1500s, and the *pampas* of Argentina, one of the richest farming and ranching areas in the world.

Latin America has changed dramatically since the days when the ancient farmers tended their lowland and highland crops. The great capital city where the Aztec emperor Montezuma ruled supreme is long gone. In its place stands Mexico City, a city of markets, skyscrapers, and slums—a bustling but polluted and overcrowded city. Most Latin Americans now speak Spanish, the language of the **conquistadors**. And most are Roman Catholics, like the priests who came with the conquerors. But the old ways and customs live on. Many Native Americans speak the tongue of their ancestors. And even with the seemingly never-ending flow of people from countryside to city, half of the population are still *campesinos*, who live and work on the land.

*conquistadors:* leaders in the Spanish conquest of the Americas

Mexican citizens carry pots of colorful flowers to church. More than three-fourths of the people of Latin America are Catholic.

In this unit natives and others tell about the life and landscape in Mexico, Central America, and South America.

- ☐ Judith Friedlander, who lived among native villagers in rural **Mexico,** describes a typical day in the life of one family.
- ☐ Mayan Ignacio Bizarro Ujpán tells of his struggle to support his family in a rural area of **Guatemala**.
- ☐ Edwin McDowell shares the memory of a trip that he and his son took through the Amazon rain forest of **Brazil**.
- ☐ In an excerpt from his *Memoirs*, the poet Pablo Neruda writes about his escape from **Chile** through the **Andes Mountains**.

# A Mexican Family

" They are expected to sweep the front yard with two homemade brooms. . . ."

**Judith Friedlander**

Small villages dot the mountainous countryside of Mexico. Three-fourths of Mexico is 1,500 feet or more above sea level.

*Nahuatl:* group of native Mexicans; descendants of the people living in Mexico before the Spanish arrived

*Doña Zeferina Barreto:* a 65-year-old woman, head of the house and twice widowed

*Doña Juana:* Rafael's second wife, 32 years old and mother of six

*Rafael:* Doña Zeferina's oldest son, a 43-year-old teacher

*tortillas:* flat round bread made from cornmeal

*chiles:* a type of hot pepper

*Don José:* Doña Zeferina's third husband

**A**nthropologist Judith Friedlander wanted to study life in rural Mexico. To do this, she lived with a **Nahuatl** family in Hueyapan from 1969 to 1970. Hueyapan is a small village near Cuernavaca, southwest of Mexico City. During the time she lived with the family and on visits over the next four years, she recorded and wrote about what she saw. In this reading she follows some of the members of the family of **Doña Zeferina Barreto** through a typical day. ∽

**Doña Juana** is the first to rise. It is about 6:30 A.M. . . . She silently puts on a cotton dress, a cotton apron and plastic shoes. Then wrapping herself up in a cotton *rebozo* (shawl), she hurries out into the brisk morning air. Juana is in a rush because she wants to beat the long lines that will soon be forming at Don Reyes Maya's corn mill. Since the corn was prepared yesterday, all Juana has to do now is fill a bucket with the *nixtamal*, as the cooked corn is called, and go to the mill, which, conveniently, is just next door. As far as Juana is concerned, it is well worth the twenty *centavos* (equivalent to two cents in U.S. currency) to have the corn ground at the mill. She vividly remembers . . . how every morning her "poor mother" had to spend a couple of hours on her knees grinding corn. . . .

After the corn is ground Juana returns to the kitchen to get the fires going. Then she puts two pots of water on to heat, one for the coffee and another for **Rafael**, who insists on having hot water to wash and shave with. Next the beans, prepared the day before, are reheated and the metal *comal* (griddle), used for cooking the **tortillas**, is washed down with water and lime (the mineral product, not the fruit). Once everything is under way in the kitchen, Juana goes to the backyard to cut a few **chiles** for the hot sauce she will serve with the beans. All that is left to do now is to make the *tortillas*, a time-consuming job for this large family.

**Don José** rises a little after Juana. . . . Silently the old man goes out to begin his early morning chore —fetching drinking water from the

20

stream at the bottom of one of the *barrancas* (gorges) that surround the village. . . .

Next to make their morning appearances are **Raúl** and **Héctor**. They are expected to sweep the front yard with two homemade brooms that are always falling apart. **Reina** and **Quico** stay in bed a bit longer and play with the pillows. **Maruca** slips out of **Rosa's** bed and joins her younger siblings in their parents' bed. Soon, however, they all want to get up and they call Rosa to come take charge of little Quico.

By this time, the little boy has begun to cry, tearfully demanding his morning piece of bread. Rosa takes Quico to the kitchen, where Juana quiets his **insistent** plea for *"pan, pan"* by giving the little fellow a twenty-*centavo* piece. Rosa then carries the cranky child down to the corner store to purchase him his bread—a sweet roll.

Next **Angelina** rises to heat up a bottle of milk for **Lilia**. . . .

Except for Lilia and **Arturo**, Doña Zeferina is the last to rise. She has been awake, however, since Don José got up, but as she told me many times, it was too cold to bother leaving her bed any earlier. Since it is Tuesday, market day in Hueyapan, and she will therefore be selling in the plaza, Doña Zeferina plans to put on a clean dress and apron instead of what she has been wearing for the past few days. . . .

While Doña Zeferina slowly washes herself, combs and braids her hair and changes her clothes, Don José, Arturo, Rosa, Raúl and Héctor carry the innumerable boxes of merchandise to the plaza. Soon the 9:00 bell rings. Rosa, Raúl and Héctor dash off to join the other pupils in front of the school.

Just as the children file into their respective classrooms, Doña Zeferina turns the corner of her street, Calle Morelos, and **majestically** walks up to her selling post in the market. Over one arm she carries a straw basket in which she keeps some change, and in her hand she holds a small scale used to weigh the chiles. Passing other vendors, Doña Zeferina stops to greet them and to see what there is to buy today.

Finally she arrives at her spot. Arturo and some of the preschool grandchildren are there waiting for her. Doña Zeferina and Arturo set about systematically arranging first the chiles, then the kitchenware and the toys, in a particular order which never varies from week to week. Doña Zeferina also attaches some plastic sheets to the awning that covers her selling area in order to protect herself from the sun. By 9:30 she is settled and the long day formally begins. . . .

By noon Juana and Angelina have finished the morning chores.

This woman is making tortillas for her family. She pats the corn dough into thin, round cakes and cooks them on a hot griddle.

*Raúl* (age 10), *Héctor* (age 8), and *Quico* (age 2) are Juana and Rafael's sons; *Rosa* (age 12), *Maruca* (age 6), and *Reina* (age 4) are their daughters.

*insistent:* demanding

*pan:* bread

*Angelina:* (age 28) only daughter and youngest child of Doña Zeferina.

*Lilia:* Angelina's daughter

*Arturo:* (age 14) Rafael's son from his first marriage

*majestically:* like a queen

Beds have been made, bedrooms and kitchen swept clean, all the breakfast dishes washed and the dogs and pigs fed. Angelina goes to the plaza to pick up the **kilo** of beef that Doña Zeferina purchased for the afternoon meal. . . .

When school lets out at 2:00, lunch is ready. The children drift home one by one and ask to be fed, each **brusquely** demanding, *"Mamá, dame de comer."* Juana complies, giving the younger children tiny portions of beans and morsels of meat. . . . Angelina is also among the first to eat, for she has to go the plaza to relieve Doña Zeferina temporarily for a lunch break. . . .

At 3:30 those people who came to sell in the plaza from villages on the Hueyapan-Cuautla bus route pack up their goods and cram into the blue and red Estrella Roja (Red Star) bus line's second-class vehicle. By this time most visitors from neighboring **pueblos** within walking distance of Hueyapan have also left for home. Only the local people

remain in the market, and in another hour and a half they too return to their houses. Doña Zeferina is one of the last to leave the market, for it takes her and Arturo a long time to repack all the toys and kitchenware. At 5:30 Don José, Arturo and a few younger children drag the cartons home again and tuck them away for another week, under Doña Zeferina's bed and in the corners of the store-room off the kitchen. . . .

By the time Doña Zeferina returns . . . it is about 6:30. . . .

The family goes into the kitchen to have a light supper of beans, reheated *tortillas* and coffee. Although it has been a hectic day, everybody is in lively spirits. . . .

The mood is **infectious**. Maruca, whose strong personality is often compared with that of her grandmother, begins to tease her older brother Héctor. Amused by her granddaughter, Doña Zeferina joins in and sings a song to Maruca, the one that always makes the little girl scream and run out of the room. . . .

*kilo:* kilogram (about 2.2 pounds)

*brusquely:* bluntly

*Mamá, dame de comer:* Mama, give me food.

*pueblos:* villages

*infectious:* catching

On market days many people gather at open-air stalls to shop for food, clothing, and household goods.

Sunlight filters through the brightly colored quilts that serve as walls in this Mexican home. Many homes have only one or two rooms.

One by one the older children leave the kitchen to go to sleep. Rosa is the last of the young people to retire, because she must wash the supper dishes before joining her brothers and sisters. Finally by about 10:00 the **bathers** have finished and they too cross over to the bedrooms and turn in for the night. Juana remains behind a few minutes longer than the rest to turn off the lights, fetch Quico from the cradle and lock the kitchen and storeroom doors with wooden bars. . . .

Then the house is silent as everyone drifts off to sleep.

*bathers:* the children who had taken baths before bed

Most Mexican villages and towns have a marketplace where people buy and sell goods. Some people bring goods such as clothes, prepared food, lace, and toys to sell or trade. Farmers bring their crops. In the marketplace, goods are openly displayed in rented booths or on the ground. Going to market is also a time for seeing and talking to friends. The markets remain an important part of the social life in small Mexican towns.

# The Life of a Maya

" . . . I woke up worrying about my poverty, my family, and what I could do to provide for them. "

**Ignacio Bizarro Ujpán**

Stone pyramids and temples still stand in the ancient Mayan city of Tikal in Guatemala.

**M**ayas make up more than half the population of Guatemala. The Mayas are a group of people native to Central America and southeastern Mexico. They had an old and highly developed civilization when they were discovered by European explorers early in the sixteenth century. In this reading one Maya, Ignacio Bizarro Ujpán, tells of his struggle to support his family. Ujpán rents small plots of land, where he grows corn and beans. He also does any available odd jobs. While many Mayas live like Ujpán and his family, others have found jobs in bigger towns and cities. ∽

*measles:* a viral disease that kills many children in poor countries

*San José :* the small town in Guatemala near the Pacific Ocean where Ignacio and his family live

*recuperate:* become well again

*remote:* far off and isolated

*A New Baby but Illness Strikes Again*

On February 10, 1972, about two weeks after I returned from the coast, my wife, Josefa, gave birth to a beautiful baby boy whom we named Ramón S. Antonio. Shortly thereafter, while my wife was still bedridden with infant Ramón, my other two little children, José and María, came down with a severe case of the **measles**.

By the grace of God I had a little money to spend because I had just returned from working on the coast. I spent some $60 without hesitation because the measles are dangerous. We well remembered little Juan Martín and little Ana María dying with this horrible disease.

We were terribly worried that little José and María might die also, but just when we were the most desperate by the grace of God two doctors, Señor Antonio Gómez Velásquez and Señor Mendoza, arrived to check on the people of **San José**.

I had spent all of my money on medicine, and I did not have any to pay the doctors. Fortunately, they only charged me 25 cents for their services, and they gave my two children injections and left pills for them to take without charging me anything. My prayers had been answered because gradually my two children began to **recuperate**. . . .

They say that doctors are supposed to visit **remote** towns such as San José and San Martín every eight days. But sometimes they are only able to come once or twice a month.

24

In any case, these doctors came when I needed them most. Indeed, it was they who saved the lives of my two children! . . .

### *Subsistence Farming* with My Family on the Farm San José Del Carmen

On April 5, 1972, I returned to the . . . farm San José del Carmen. But this time I went to work for myself, and I took my family along, except my little daughter María, who stayed with my wife's mother.

When we arrived at the farm, I went to ask the administrator for land to rent for planting corn. He said that he would pay for the lease on the land if I would plant livestock pasture (or grass for cattle) for him in return.

I began to work the next day, but since we only had $3 for expenses such as food, I had to work some of the days as a **day laborer**. In all I planted nine *cuerdas* of corn. We stayed 35 days on the farm until after I had finished the second **cleaning** of the field.

On May 10, we got up at 2:00 A.M. and set out walking back to San José. I carried all of our kitchen utensils and clothing on my back. Most of the time I also carried José because he was too small to walk very much. By the time we reached San Luis at noon, we were exhausted. We had walked all of the way. In San Luis we boarded a large canoe to San Martín, and from there we walked to San José. It had been a long, tiring trip.

Eight days later I returned for 20 days more on the coast to clean the cornfield again. Once more, I planted pasture for the cows to pay for renting the land.

I returned to San José on June 5, during the **patron fiesta** of the town. For us the fiesta was not a happy time for we had no money to celebrate. For the next two weeks I worked as a *jornalero* whenever I could find work. Usually, one can earn 50 cents a day as a *jornalero*, but during the harvest season, there is more work, and it is possible to make as much as

*subsistence farming:* raising only enough crops to feed one's family

*day laborer:* unskilled laborer who works for daily wages

*cuerdas:* Spanish measurement. A cuerda equals about 30 feet.

*cleaning:* weeding

*patron fiesta:* festival of the special saint, or patron

*jornalero:* day laborer

Mayan men bind bundles of reeds to make roofs for their homes. Homes usually have dirt floors and only one or two rooms. Mats or hammocks are used for sleeping.

75 cents a day. Of course, I had to work at something to support my family.

I began to think that nine *cuerdas* of corn would be more than my family needed, and on June 21, I went to offer three *cuerdas* to my father-in-law. He agreed to buy them at $15 a *cuerda* so he paid me $45. I used this money to buy necessities for my family. During this period, my family and I suffered a lot because of our extreme poverty! . . .

*Poverty, **Insomnia**, and Illnesses*
*August 8-9, 1972*

At 3:00 A.M. I woke up worrying about my poverty, my family, and what I could do to provide for them. My worry caused sleeplessness. I finally got out of bed without having slept much, gave thanks to God, and ate a **meager** breakfast.

During the morning I cleaned weeds from my *cuerda* of beans, stopping at noon to eat my lunch of tortillas and beans with salt. All I had to drink was a bottle of piped water. While I ate, I thought how sad and hard the life of a poor man is!

I finished my chores in the field at 3:00 P.M., and I went home to rest. I was **ravenous**, and my wife prepared dinner. After eating, to relax I opened the book *The Towns of Lake Atitlán* that my good friend Jaime had given me as a remembrance. I didn't stop reading this interesting book about the native towns where I live until 9:00 P.M. By this time it was getting too dark to read by candlelight, and besides my eyes were tired.

When I got up the next morning at 6:00 A.M., I asked my wife to fix breakfast for me, but she was unable to get out of bed. Because she had a fever, she could not cook. Thus, I fixed breakfast for my children and myself.

I debated over whether I should go to work in the fields, but I finally was too concerned about my wife's being sick. Instead of going to hoe, I went to the public health center in San José to ask for medicine. Because I had no money, I could not go to a pharmacy.

After fixing lunch for the children at noon, I went with the Peruvian to interview two Protestant families about their reasons for changing religion. I got home around 6:30, and I prepared dinner because my wife was still too sick to work. . . .

*Thinking of My Children's Future*
*September 28, 1976*

After breakfast I took my little son Ramón Antonio to work with me in Tamalaj where I have a little coffee grove. It is just 200 **matas**, but when the trees are big they will help me with my expenses. Because I have not had time to clean the grove, there was a lot of growth.

For the first time my little son Ramón ate lunch while working in

**insomnia:** sleeplessness

**meager:** very small

**ravenous:** very hungry

**matas:** sprigs

Many Mayan women wear long skirts, head coverings, and sashes woven by hand from brightly colored fibers.

Although the Guatemalan government provides free schooling, attendance at the schools is low. Many Mayan children stay at home to help on the family farms.

the fields. We had tortillas and *chipilín*. My little son is learning about working in the fields. But I want my children to have an education so that when they are grown they will not have to live the kind of life that I have. My life is full of suffering. I am intelligent, but I don't have a sixth-grade diploma. Nowadays with a sixth-grade diploma one can get work. It is possible to get a diploma by **conspiring** to give the heads of the institutions $100. But I don't have this kind of money to give for a diploma because my family expenses are high.

*chipilín:*
wild greens

*conspiring:*
joining in an illegal agreement (here used to mean bribing)

Life continues to be hard for many Mayas such as Ujpán. Poverty is widespread among the native people in rural Guatemala. Lack of education is one cause of this poverty. Most of the rural Mayas cannot read or write. Few teachers in Guatemala, however, can speak the Mayan languages. Many Mayas, like Ujpán, see education as a way for their children to live better lives.

From *Son of Tecún Umán*, ed. James D. Sexton (Tucson: University of Arizona Press, 1981), pp. 75–77, 82–83, 204. Reprinted by permission.

# The Magical Rain Forest

"... I tried to impart to Eddie some of my own love for the Amazon. ..."

**Edwin McDowell**

The Amazon River carries more water than any river in the world and is second only to the Nile in length.

piranha:
meat-eating fish

resolve:
determination

inoculations:
shots to prevent
certain diseases

cavort: play

grandeur: greatness

impart: give

iguanas:
large lizards

Paleolithic Age:
early historic period
during which
primitive human
beings made and
used stone tools

flora: plant life

Salvador Dali:
modern Spanish
painter who painted
scenes from
imaginary worlds

The Amazon River flows 4,000 miles through Peru and Brazil. Its waters are home to unique fish such as the fierce **piranha.** Alligators, parrots, and sloths are among the many animals that live on its banks. The rain forest that surrounds the Amazon River contains more than 40,000 kinds of plants. Some can be found nowhere else in the world. Author Edwin McDowell tells of his son Eddie's first trip to the Amazon River.

He who travels alone may indeed travel fastest, but I can think of little else to recommend solitary travel. In nearly a dozen trips to the Amazon, my Brazilian-born wife had accompanied me only once, and we had more or less agreed that I would wait until our son, Eddie, turned 12 before I exposed him to the potential hazards of the adventure. But my impatience to share the Amazon's beauty with my son weakened my **resolve**, and after specialists in tropical medicine told me simply to follow normal precautions, I decided to take him with me on a recent trip when he was only 8. He agreed to submit to the necessary **inoculations** if I would let him fish for piranhas.

A few weeks later we stood side by side on the deck of a riverboat watching freshwater dolphins **cavort** off our bow. And for the next three weeks, journeying nearly a thousand miles into the Brazilian Amazon, we shared each other's wonder at the **grandeur** and mystery of one of the world's last frontiers.

As I tried to **impart** to Eddie some of my own love for the Amazon, I began to see familiar sights through the eyes of youth, as though I were entering this magical rain forest for the first time. Standing on the lower level of a double-decker Amazon boat, we glided by several motionless **iguanas**, looking like props for a movie set in the **Paleolithic Age** as they sunned themselves. ... We counted 11 distinct shades of green in the **flora** along just one small section of the riverbank. And everywhere we went we saw fish as big as men, butterflies as big as birds and birds that looked as if they had been painted by **Salvador Dali.**

Because it was Eddie's first visit, I devised an **itinerary** that would allow him to enjoy the major attractions in the cities and still be able to spend enough time in the jungle to appreciate the life and color that abound there. . . .

In my solitary travels I have met an endless assortment of drifters and dreamers, preachers and **prospectors**, soldiers and **soldiers of fortune**. But having my son along soon taught me how much I had missed. Everywhere we went, strangers took an immediate liking to Eddie, and when they discovered that he speaks excellent Portuguese they went out of their way to make us welcome.

A school principal, for example, showed my son the lengthy trails **wrought** through the jungle by leaf-cutter ants and the many spikes that protrude from beneath the leaves of a common palm tree. . . . The security guard at the **Teatro da Paz in Belém**, after taking us on a private tour through the theater's crystal and **gilt** interior, turned on the footlights and encouraged my son to stand center stage, where **Anna Pavlova** and **Jascha Heifetz** once performed, while I snapped photographs. . . .

Later on, I watched with mixed emotions as my son joined a dozen other children his age during their nightly swim in the Amazon—not 200 yards from the reef where at that very hour a Brazilian employee of the school caught a foot-long piranha.

The piranhas kept their distance while my son swam, not just in the Amazon, but in the Rio Negro and the Tapajós. But when we fished for them near Santarém, I learned that their **ferocity** is not just the stuff of Hollywood legend. The two of us and three new friends—a young couple from **Geneva** and a young man from **São Paulo**—set out up the Amazon by boat. . . . The piranhas were so

*itinerary:* travel plan

*prospectors:* people who look for riches

*soldiers of fortune:* military persons willing to serve anywhere for adventure or money

*wrought:* made

*Teatro da Paz in Belém:* theater in Belém, a city in northern Brazil

*gilt:* gold-covered

*Anna Pavlova:* a Russian ballerina

*Jascha Heifetz:* an American violinist, born in Russia

*ferocity:* fierceness

*Geneva:* city in Switzerland

*São Paulo:* largest city in Brazil

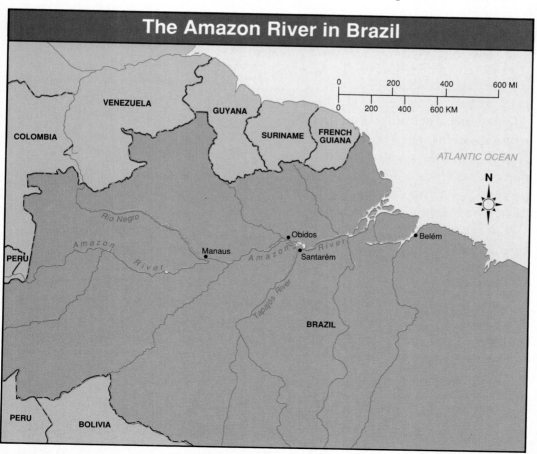

## The Amazon River in Brazil

VENEZUELA
GUYANA
COLOMBIA
SURINAME
FRENCH GUIANA
ATLANTIC OCEAN
N
PERU
Rio Negro
Amazon River
Manaus
Obidos
Santarém
Amazon River
Belém
Tapajós River
BRAZIL
PERU
BOLIVIA

0  200  400  600 MI
0  200  400  600 KM

Instead of traveling by foot through the dense Amazon jungle, many people travel by river in dugout canoes.

*cove:* small sheltered bay

*samba:* Brazilian dance

*plied:* continuously presented or gave

*rustic:* primitive

*benefactors:* people who give gifts

*idyllic:* peaceful

*lepers:* people who have leprosy (a deforming skin disease)

*gringo:* non-Hispanic person

*famously:* very well

abundant in the **cove** where we tied up that it was only a matter of dropping a line into the water before they struck the hooks baited with pieces of raw meat. The trick was landing them: a dozen wriggled off the hooks onto the deck, each time setting off a frenzied **samba** among passengers and crew. But the most dramatic moment occurred when a crew member picked up the piranha that my son had caught and thrust a wedge of ice up to its jaws. Almost immediately, the piranha slashed at the ice with its razorlike teeth, sending chips flying in every direction. . . .

Everywhere we went, strangers **plied** Eddie with gifts. A shopkeeper in Obidos gave him a slingshot made completely of rubber. A young woman in an arts-and-crafts shop in Belém gave him a **rustic** flute hand-carved by Indians, and threw in a 10-minute music lesson. A photographer we befriended in

Manaus, who was raised deep in the jungle near the Bolivian border, kept my son spellbound with the assorted whistles, trills and clicks by which he mimicked the sounds of birds and jungle creatures. In return, we gave our **benefactors** postcards of New York, which they unfailingly asked us to autograph.

Our journey was not completely **idyllic**, to be sure, because the jungle is not idyllic—at least not for those who live there. My son viewed with fascination and horror the many **lepers** that I had long taken for granted. And in the bigger cities he saw the abandoned children—there are an estimated seven million in Brazil alone—who are the tragedy of most South American countries. "Where are their parents?" Eddie asked one night. "Why do they sleep outside instead of in beds?" I could offer no adequate explanation. . . .

Our last day and night in the Amazon were something I had been looking forward to for several years —the opportunity to introduce my son to Robin McGighn, a resident of Belém who settled in the Amazon in 1944 and never left. At the age of 84, he is still active as a consultant on Amazon wood and forest products, and he still burns with the jungle fever that gets into the blood of many people who see the Amazon for the first time. . . .

Today, he is as close as any **gringo** can be to being a legend in the eastern Amazon. So I wanted my son, who like most kids his age has grown up with television's superheroes, to meet a living legend. More than that, I wanted him to meet a man who has never abandoned his youthful dream.

They hit it off **famously**, as I was sure they would. Even now it is difficult to describe the pleasure I felt at seeing Robin, somewhat stooped with age but still over 6 feet tall, holding hands with my 4-foot 6-inch son on the way to dinner, during a tour of a lumber mill or just walking down the street. Although separated in age by more than three-quarters of a century, they were inseparable during our brief time together.

When we parted, Robin gave us both a traditional **abraço** and, with tears in his eyes, said to Eddie, "God bless you, son. And come back to the Amazon."

"Will you still be here?" my son asked in all innocence.

I **blanched** at the question, but Robin just smiled. "Why sure I'll still be here," he said. "But what really matters is that the Amazon will be here. It will be here long after all of us."

*abraço:* hug

*blanched:* turned pale

Ferries and cargo boats dock at the Amazon port of Manaus in Brazil. Houses are built on stilts to protect them from rising water.

The rain forest along the Amazon River is the largest in the world. Many sections of the forest have never been disturbed by human beings. In some places, however, people have cleared away the forest for logging, farming, ranching, and oil exploration. Conservationists think that 20 percent of the rain forest may already be destroyed. They fear that the unique Amazon rain forest may someday disappear. Many organizations around the world are working to preserve the rain forest.

From Edwin McDowell, "River Wonderland: An 8-Year-Old Discovers the Amazon," *The Sophisticated Traveler* (March 16, 1986), pp. 65, 86, 89, 94. Copyright © 1986 by The New York Times Company. Reprinted by permission.

# Andes Escape

> " There was something waiting for us in that wild forest. "
>
> **Pablo Neruda**

The jagged snow-capped peaks of the Andes extend the full length of South America's western coast.

*passes:* places where a mountain range can be crossed

*smugglers:* people who transport goods illegally

*precipices:* edges of cliffs

*surveyor:* person who measures land

*Aconcagua:* the highest mountain in the Andes and the Western Hemisphere; located in western Argentina near the Chilean border

*coniferous:* cone-bearing evergreen

*girth:* distance around the trunk

*humus:* part of soil made of decomposed plants and animals

*flimsiest:* weakest

Crossing the boundary to another country can be a physical challenge. The rugged Andes Mountains in South America form the border between Chile and Argentina. Pablo Neruda, a poet and politician in Chile, had to cross the Andes. When he criticized the new government in 1948, orders went out for his arrest. Neruda fled the country on horseback. He crossed the Andes Mountains in order to reach safety in Argentina.

The Andean mountains have hidden **passes**, used by **smugglers** in the old days, so hostile and difficult that the rural police no longer bother to patrol them. Rivers and **precipices** block the traveler's way.

My companion Jorge Bellet headed the expedition. Our five-man escort, expert horsemen and road scouts, was joined by my old friend Victor Bianchi, who had come to the region as **surveyor** in some land disputes. He did not recognize me. I had a heavy beard after a year and a half of living in hiding. As soon as he knew about my plan to cross the jungle, he offered us his invaluable services as veteran explorer. He had once climbed **Aconcagua** on a tragic expedition in which he had been one of the only survivors.

We traveled single-file, protected by the solemn hour of dawn. I had not ridden a horse in many years, not since childhood, but here we were, on our way to the pass. The southern Andean forest is populated by huge trees set apart from one another: giant larches and mayten trees, as well as tepa and **coniferous** trees. The rauli trees have an amazing **girth**. I stopped to measure one. It had the diameter of a horse. The sky overhead can't be seen. Below, leaves have been falling for centuries, forming a layer of **humus** the hoofs of the mounts sink down into. We were passing through one of primitive nature's great cathedrals.

Our way took us through hidden and forbidden territory, and we accepted even the **flimsiest** indications we could follow. There were no tracks, no trails; my four mounted companions and I wove in and out, overcoming such obstacles as powerful trees, impassable rivers, enormous **crags**, **desolate snows**, guessing more often than not, looking for the road to my freedom. My companions were sure of their bearings, the best way between the thick clumps of vegetation, but, to be on the safe side, they **notched** the bark of the huge trees here and there with a **machete**, blazing a trail to guide them back, once they had left me to my fate.

Each one moved along, absorbed in that solitude without boundary lines. . . .

Sometimes we followed a dim trail left by smugglers perhaps or by common outlaws fleeing from justice; we wondered how many had **perished**, surprised by winter's icy hand, in the heavy snowstorms that break loose in the Andes and surround the traveler, burying him under seven stories of snow. . . .

We had to cross a river. Those small springs born on the Andean peaks **plummet** down, unload their **vertiginous**, crushing power, turn into waterfalls, tear up land and rocks with the energy and speed gathered in those staggering altitudes.

But this time we came upon a pool, a huge mirror of water, a **ford**. The horses went in, lost their footing, and swam to the other side. My mount was soon almost totally covered by the water, I began to sway unsteadily, my drifting feet thrashed about, while the animal struggled to keep its head above water. So we went across. And no sooner had we reached the other shore than my guides, the peasants who accompanied me, grinned and asked: "Were you very scared?"

"Very. I thought my end had come," I replied.

"We were behind you with a rope ready in our hands," they said.

"My father fell in right there," one of them added, "and the current dragged him away. We weren't about to let the same thing happen to you."

We went on, eventually entering a natural tunnel opened in the impressive rock perhaps by a powerful river that has since disappeared or by a **spasm** of the earth that created this formation in the mountains, dug this canal in the **hinterlands**, **excavated** from the rock, the granite which we

*crags:* steep rugged rocks

*desolate snows:* bare snowfields

*notched:* made cuts in

*machete:* large heavy knife

*perished:* died

*plummet:* fall a great distance

*vertiginous:* dizzying

*ford:* relatively shallow, calm place that can be crossed in a river

*spasm:* violent shake, used here to mean earthquake

*hinterlands:* region far from civilization

*excavated:* carved out

Water from the melting snow in the Andes flows swiftly down the mountains and over cliffs to create powerful waterfalls such as Laja Falls in central Chile.

Modern Chilean cowboys, called *huasos*, still wear traditional wide-brimmed hats, leather chaps, and brightly colored ponchos to herd cattle in the flatlands.

*grueling:* physically exhausting

*crystalline:* extremely clear, like a crystal

*foliage:* leaves

*Ulysses:* a leader of the ancient Greeks who wandered the world for ten years before returning home

*fugitives:* people who run away or escape

*gorges:* narrow canyons

*ramshackle:* broken down

*curdled:* made into cheese

were now entering. A little farther on, the mounts kept slipping, they would try to get a footing in the rocky depressions, their legs buckled, sparks flew from their shoes. I was thrown from my horse and sprawled out on the rocks more than once. My horse was bleeding at the nose and legs, but we stubbornly continued on our vast, magnificent, **grueling** way.

There was something waiting for us in that wild forest. Suddenly we came out into a neat little meadow, an unbelievable vision, nestled in the mountain's lap: **crystalline** water, green grass, wild flowers, the murmur of streams, and a blue sky over us, a generous light unbroken by **foliage**.

We stopped inside this magic circle, like guests in a holy place: and even holier was the ceremony in which I took part. The cowboys dismounted. A bull's skull had been set down in the center of the hollow, as if for some ritual. My companions approached it in silence, one by one, and left a few coins and some food in its bone sockets. I joined them in that offering intended for rough-mannered men who had strayed away like **Ulysses**, for **fugitives** of every breed, who would find bread and assistance in the dead bull's eyepits. . . .

Farther along, that night, just before we were to cross the frontier that would separate me from my country for many years, we came to the last mountain **gorges**. Suddenly we saw a burning light, a sure sign of human life, and coming closer, we found several **ramshackle** sheds that looked empty. We entered one of them and saw, by the firelight, huge logs burning in the center of the room, bodies of giant trees that burned there day and night, releasing, through cracks in the roof, smoke that drifted in the dark like a heavy blue veil. We saw piles of cheeses, stacked there by those who had **curdled** them at that altitude. Several men, huddled together like sacks, were lying next to the fire. . . . They didn't know who we were, they knew nothing about the fugitive, they didn't know my poetry or my name. Or did they know it, did they know us? Anyway, we sang and ate next to that fire, and later we walked through the dark into some crude rooms. A thermal spring passed through them, volcanic water we plunged into, a warmth that broke from the mountains and drew us close to itself.

We splashed around happily, washing, cleansing off the heaviness of our long ride. We felt refreshed, born again, baptized, when we set out at dawn on the final kilometers that would take me away from the **shadows hovering over my country**. We left on our horses, singing, with a new air filling our lungs, a breath that drove us on to the great highway of the world waiting for me. When we tried—this is still fresh in my mind—to give the mountaineers some money to pay for the songs, the food, the thermal waters, the bed and the roof, that is, for the unexpected welcome we had met, they refused our offer without even considering it. They had done what they could for us, that's all. And "that's all," the silent "that's all," **implied** many things, perhaps recognition, perhaps our common dreams.

*shadows hovering over my country:* political problems in Chile

*implied:* suggested

People who live in the Andes have been slow to change their old ways. They are isolated from the large cities by the rugged landscape. Roads are expensive and difficult to build.

After escaping from Chile, Pablo Neruda visited Europe and the Soviet Union. He then lived in Mexico. Neruda wrote some of his best-known poetry during this time. When the government of Chile lifted his arrest order in 1952, he returned to Chile. There he continued to write as well as work in politics. In 1971 Neruda was awarded the **Nobel Prize** for Literature. Many of his poems are about his homeland.

*Nobel Prize:* a yearly prize given to people who do great work for the good of humanity; named after the Swedish scientist Alfred Nobel

Excerpt from *Memoirs* by Pablo Neruda, translated by Hardie St. Martin, pp. 180–84.
Translation copyright © 1976, 1977 by Farrar, Straus and Giroux, Inc.

# WESTERN EUROPE

*Scandinavian Peninsula:* large peninsula made up of Norway and Sweden

*Iberian Peninsula:* peninsula made up of Spain and Portugal

In and out it snakes, the jagged coastline of Western Europe. The coast twists and turns and winds around, forming one peninsula after another—the **Scandinavian Peninsula** in the north, the **Iberian Peninsula** in the southwest, boot-shaped Italy, and Greece. Deep bays, well-protected inlets, narrow gulfs, and picture-perfect harbors define this coastline. And off the coasts lie hundreds of islands, ranging from island nations such as Iceland and Ireland to tiny, rocky Greek islands where no one lives.

Within Western Europe rolling plains and waterways seem to be everywhere. The Arctic Ocean, the Mediterranean Sea, and the Atlantic Ocean all lap at the shores of this small region. Rivers course through its interior and flow through broad and fertile plains. The Great European Plain is the largest of these. A sweep of flat and rolling land, the Great European Plain cuts a wide path from southern Britain in the west, across northern France, Belgium, the Netherlands, and West Germany, and into the Soviet Union. On this great plain are Western Europe's biggest and most glittering cities, most of its people, and most of its agriculture and industry.

The rivers of Western Europe have always been a lifeline. In the past commerce and communication revolved around the rivers because they were the easiest way to travel. Of the many grand rivers of Western

Europe, none is as busy or as important as the Rhine. From the high peaks of the Swiss Alps it winds hundreds of miles through Switzerland, Austria, Germany, France, and the Netherlands to the North Sea. Flat-bottomed barges, giant cargo ships, slender sailboats, and sightseeing craft loaded with tourists are all carried along by the Rhine, which has the heaviest river traffic in Europe.

The Alps, where the Rhine comes to life, is the major mountain range of Western Europe and covers parts of six countries. The crystal clear lakes there reflect forests and snow-capped peaks. Flocks of sheep and cattle graze in high meadows, farms nestle in the deep green valleys, and lakeside and mountaintop resorts attract skiers and hikers. High in the Alps, it is hard to remember the dusty sunny plains and hills of the Mediterranean countries or the cool, moist climate and green, gentle land of Great Britain.

No matter which country Western Europeans live in, they can see reminders of their rich history every day. Ancient Greek temples and roads built by the Romans still remain. **Medieval** castles and cathedrals abound. Most of the land and climate of Western Europe is so **hospitable** that it has been a densely populated region for many centuries. As a consequence, everywhere in the landscape, from the industrialized cities to the rural villages, there are echoes of the glories and sorrows of the past.

*medieval:* of the Middle Ages, European era from about A.D. 500 to 1500

*hospitable:* pleasant and comfortable; supplying needs

Many countries in Western Europe depend on the sea for transportation, food, and jobs. These Greek women prepare nets for a day of fishing.

The readings in this unit cover some of the economic, cultural, and natural characteristics of Western Europe.

- ■ The eighteenth-century scientist Carolus Linnaeus describes in his journal the climate, vegetation, and landforms in **Lapland**.
- ☐ Alfred Alvarez talks with the workers who drill for oil from platforms in the **North Sea**.
- ■ In a letter to a friend, the Roman writer Pliny gives an eyewitness account of the eruption of Mount Vesuvius in **Italy** in A.D. 79.
- ■ After traveling in **Greece**, American Jesse Stuart tells of his visit to the site of the first Olympic games.

# My Lapland Journey

**Linnaeus**

Carol Linnaeus, a Swedish botanist and explorer, developed a scientific system for naming plants and animals.

Although most of Western Europe has a mild climate, the area above the Arctic Circle in Norway, Sweden, and Finland is very cold. This area is known as Lapland. High in the mountains of Lapland, the air stays cold all year. Snow covers the mountaintops even in summer. Farther down the mountains, the air is warmer and plants thrive. In 1732 the Swedish scientist Carolus Linnaeus spent three months collecting plants in Lapland. His journal tells of his trip.

*lofty:* high

*elevation:* height

*perpetual:* constant; without interruption

*yielded:* given in

*chasm:* deep crack

*strata:* layers

*chilblains:* itching and swelling of hands or feet caused by exposure to cold

*precipice:* steep cliff

*torrents:* violent rushing streams of water

*betwixt:* between

*July 11, 1732*

We rose early this morning, and after walking a quarter of a mile arrived at the **lofty** icy mountain. This is indeed of a very great **elevation**, and covered with **perpetual** snow, the surface of which was, for the most part, frozen quite hard. Sometimes we walked firmly over it, but it occasionally gave way, crumbling under our feet like sand. Every now and then we came to a river taking its course under the snowy crust, which in some parts had **yielded** to the force of the currents, and the sides of each **chasm** exhibited many snowy **strata** one above another. Here the mountain streams began to take their course westward, a sign of our having reached Norwegian Lapland. . . .

The whole country was one dazzling snowy waste. The cold east wind quickened our steps, and obliged us to protect our hands that we might escape **chilblains**. I was glad to put on an additional coat. As we proceeded across the north side of this mountain, we were often so violently driven along by the force of the wind, that we were taken off our feet, and rolled a considerable way down the hill. This once happened to me in so dangerous a place, that . . . I arrived near the brink of a **precipice**, and thus my part in the drama had very nearly come to an end. The rain, which fell in **torrents** on all sides, froze on our shoes and backs into a crust of ice. . . .

At length, after having travelled **betwixt** three and four miles, the mountains appeared before us, bare

**38**

of snow though only sterile rocks, and between them we caught a view of the western ocean. . . .

Having thus **traversed** the **alps,** we arrived about noon upon their bold and **precipitous** limits to the westward. The ample forests spread out beneath us, looked like fine green fields, the loftiest trees appearing no more than herbs. . . . We now **descended** into a lower country. It seems, as I write this, that I am still walking down the mountain, so long and steep was the descent. . . . When we arrived at the plains below, how grateful was the transition from a chill and frozen mountain to a warm **balmy** valley! I sat down to **regale** myself with strawberries. Instead of ice and snow, I was surrounded with vegetation in all its prime. Such tall grass I had never before beheld in any country. Instead of the blustering wind so lately experienced, soft gales **wafted** around us the grateful scent of flowery clover and various other plants. In the earlier part of my journey, I had for some time experienced a long-continued spring . . . ; then **unremitting** winter and eternal snow surrounded me; summer at length was truly welcome. Oh how most lovely of all is summer!

*traversed:* crossed

*alps:* high rugged mountains

*precipitous:* steep

*descended:* went down

*balmy:* mild

*regale:* delight

*wafted:* floated

*unremitting:* persistent; not stopping

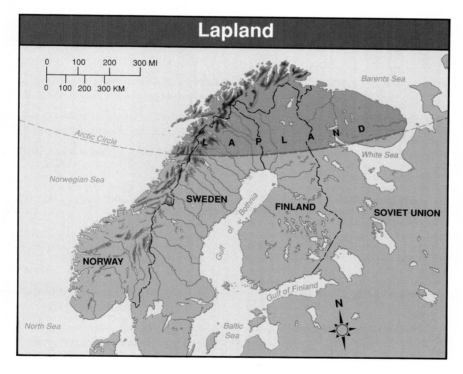

When Linnaeus visited Lapland, it was inhabited by people known as the Lapps. For thousands of years, most Lapps lived in tents and traveled from place to place with their reindeer herds. Others were fishers and fur traders. Today, most Lapps live in houses in small towns and settlements. They wear brightly colored wool clothing and reindeer skins. They mainly farm and fish for a living. Only about 10 percent of the Lapps continue to herd reindeer. They move from place to place in search of vegetation to feed their herds.

From Carl Linnaeus, *A Tour in Lapland,* ed. Robert M. Goldwyn, M.D. (reprinted, New York: Arno Press, 1971).

# Drilling for North Sea Oil

" Those crane drivers," he said. "They're real artists. "

**Alfred Alvarez**

Large oil rigs in the North Sea pump petroleum from beneath the sea floor.

**A**s one of the world's major industrial regions, Western Europe has a huge demand for energy sources. The large supplies of good-quality coal once found there have been almost depleted. Today oil and natural gas are needed. In 1969 oil was discovered under the North Sea off the east coast of Scotland. Alfred Alvarez talked to the people who work on the **oil rigs** in the North Sea. The workers describe how even the basic task of loading supplies on the offshore platform is challenging and requires great skill.

*oil rigs:* platforms holding equipment for drilling oil

*installations:* offshore oil rigs

*£60 and £80:* (60 pounds and 80 pounds) approximately $99 and $131

*Brent*: group of oil rigs in the North Sea

*Aberdeen:* port city in northern Scotland

*Shetland:* the Shetland Islands, off northern Scotland

*fifty-foot sea:* waves fifty feet tall

*Alan Jacobs:* oil platform supervisor

*stowed:* stored

*forty knots:* about 46 miles per hour

From time to time—usually in emergencies—special pieces of equipment are shipped offshore by helicopter. Everything else goes by supply boat—from the 56,948 tons of piping to the two and a half million eggs, 1015 gallons of tomato ketchup, and 970 miles of toilet paper consumed each year on Shell's northern **installations**—a total of more than half a million tons of supplies at a cost varying between **£60** and **£80** a ton.

Getting there is easy: the journey to **Brent** from Torry Docks in **Aberdeen** takes twenty-four hours, from Holmsgarth in **Shetland** a mere eight. There are only two major problems and they begin when the supply boat arrives at the platform: how to hold the vessel steady in a howling wind and a **fifty-foot sea,**

and how then to transfer the materials to the installation. "It demands very fine seamanship from the ship's master and very fine crane driving as well," said **Alan Jacobs**. "You get a load on the end of that crane; suddenly it drops fifty feet; the next moment it's coming back up at you. Backloading—transferring materials from the platform to the supply boat—is even trickier. The boat has probably been to other platforms and has containers already **stowed** on the deck. All that's left is a little square of space and maybe the wind is blowing at **forty knots**. The crane driver has to put a container down into that little square on the moving deck and let his hook go before the boat drops again. Then the deck hands have to get it lashed down double-quick because the last three deaths we've had out there have occurred when the **stern** of the boat has tipped up and an unsecured container has gone wallop. . . . Maybe half a million tons of supplies doesn't sound much, given the size of our North Sea operations. But when you consider the difficulties simply of moving the stuff on and off the platforms you get a different **perspective**." Like nearly everyone involved in the offshore world, Jacobs enjoys dazzling outsiders with the **telephone-number statistics** of the business and the **disproportionate** troubles that have to be overcome. But in some areas he, too, remains impressed. "Those crane drivers," he said. "They're real artists."

The glass-sided control cabin of the crane on **Brent Alpha** is close to the flame of the gas vent that sticks out horizontally over the sea and warms the crane driver, whatever the weather. "It's nice and cozy now," said **Gordon Bunch**. "But in summer it gets a bit **torrid**." Gordon Bunch is a **corpulent**, middle-aged man with curly hair, a soft **West Country** accent, and twenty years' experience as a crane driver—five of them in the North Sea. . . . "Your **elements**," he said when I asked him the difference between working offshore and on land. He swung the crane around until our backs were toward the gas vent and the hook was above a little slot on the platform's **superstructure**. "Wind makes a hell of a difference. We **reckon** to work up to forty knots. Occasionally, we have to go over, but it's Shell policy to stop at forty. And more than that, it's not ideal, like. You haven't got the same control. The containers spin like tops when you pick them up." A foreman stood beside the slot and patted his hands up and down as if he were playing bongo drums. Bunch moved a lever and the hook sank out of sight into the slot. He went on talking: "Besides

that, the boat is moving up and down, see, she's moving from side to side. Plus the fact that if they can't **hold her off**, she's going in and out. And that's where your **precision** comes in. You've got to hold your load over, then drop her down. But providing it's not too rough, you can square it up pretty well to where they want it. . . . In actual fact, sometimes it's quite fun when the wind's tricky and the boat's playing up. But the real difference out here is height. It doesn't matter how long you've been driving cranes, when you first come offshore and drop that hook down you're likely to be miles out. But once you get used to it, you drop your **boom** out and you know more or less exactly where the hook is going."

A supply boat had drawn up to the platform and was pitching up and down in the **boisterous** sea, waiting to unload. It was a clumsy-looking vessel, its **bridge** and crew's

Helicopter traffic is common on the large oil rigs. Helicopters transport workers and some equipment to and from land.

*stern:* rear part

*perspective:* point of view

*telephone-number statistics:* large numerical facts

*disproportionate:* more than usual

*Brent Alpha:* name of the oil platform the author is on

*Gordon Bunch:* crane driver

*torrid:* very hot

*corpulent:* heavy

*West Country:* western part of England

*elements:* weather

*superstructure:* part of the oil rig above the platform

*reckon:* plan

*hold her off:* keep the boat steady

*precision:* accuracy

*boom:* long pole used to support and move cargo

*boisterous:* rough; stormy

*bridge:* raised part of deck from which the ship is steered

quarters squeezed on top of each other in the **bow**, leaving a great flat **platypus** tail, crammed with containers. It was brand new. "Not a week old," said Bunch authoritatively. Its paintwork was gleaming **terra cotta**; its wooden deck was unmarked. "*Baldar Vigra, Oslo*" was painted on its stern.

"I'll show you what I mean," said Bunch. "I'll swing out the boom and you tell me when to drop her."

I leaned into his cabin and peered through the window while the crane rotated. The *Baldar Vigra* looked **improbably** small and far off but I thought it was worth a try. "Now," I said.

Bunch pulled a lever and the hook dropped. It landed sixty feet short of the boat's stern. "See what I mean?" said Bunch.

He brought the hook back up, **manipulated** the levers again, then lowered the hook gently until it was directly over a container in the stern. Two sailors, as **agile** and quick as monkeys in the confined space, attached the hook to cables on the container. They waved. Bunch waited, playing his line like a fisherman, watching the waves and the rolling, bucking boat. It rose and fell, rose and fell, rose again. At the precise moment when the boat was at the peak of the incoming wave, Bunch pulled a lever and the container slid clear of its narrow space. It swung up and around in a great arc, like a cannonball, than stopped suddenly, as if by word of command, a foot or so from Brent Alpha's superstructure.

"Magic," I said.

"Ah well, see, that's where your crane driving comes in," Bunch said. "The trick is to keep up with her, so you're always over her, never pulling, never letting her get ahead. It's what you call a knack."

A tugboat guides an offshore rig out to sea where it will be lifted onto supporting columns. Huge drill bits will be installed to penetrate the ocean floor.

The foreman had moved round and was now playing his drums again above the invisible equipment deck. Bunch watched him, not his levers, and the container sank out of sight. A few minutes later the foreman signaled again, Bunch manipulated the levers, and another container rose into the air from the equipment deck, swung smoothly up and around, stopped suddenly in midflight, and dropped into the first container's slot on the heaving deck of the supply boat. The deck hands **uncoupled** the hook and waved. The moment the hook was clear, the *Baldar Vigra* took off for the next stop on it's schedule.

"[Jeez]," I said.

Bunch looked pleased.

*uncoupled:* disconnected

A supply boat carrying containers of supplies and equipment approaches an offshore oil platform. Choppy seas and stormy weather sometimes make it difficult to deliver the supplies.

The oil found under the North Sea has helped boost the economy of the United Kingdom. Today, the United Kingdom is a major producer and exporter of oil. But offshore drilling is dangerous work. Workers must be on guard against high winds and sudden storms. They must stay on the platforms for weeks at a time. Because of the hardships, workers on offshore rigs are paid much more than oil workers on land.

# A Volcano Erupts!

" . . . they were still in darkness, blacker and denser than any night that ever was . . ."

**Pliny**

At least 20,000 people lived in Pompeii when Mount Vesuvius erupted, burying the city in hot ashes.

**M**ount Vesuvius is an active volcano in the Apennine mountain range in Italy. It has erupted 80 times in the past 2,000 years. The last time it erupted was in 1944. All over the world, newspapers wrote about the village that the volcano destroyed. But when Vesuvius erupted in A.D. 79, there were no newspapers to report what happened. The account that follows is from the Roman writer Pliny. He witnessed the event and described it in a letter.

*Misenum:* present-day Porto di Miseno, a city on the Bay of Naples. Misenum was a naval base at the time Pliny wrote.

*subsided:* decreased

*dispersed:* spread in different directions

*acumen:* quick understanding

*Tascius:* Roman noble

*implored:* begged

My uncle was stationed at **Misenum**, in active command of the fleet. On 24 August, in the early afternoon, my mother drew his attention to a cloud of unusual size and appearance. . . . It was not clear at that distance from which mountain the cloud was rising (it was afterwards known to be Vesuvius); its general appearance can best be expressed as being like a pine rather than any other tree, for it rose to a great height on a sort of trunk and then split off into branches, I imagine because it was thrust upwards by the first blast and then left unsupported as the pressure **subsided**, or else it was borne down by its own weight so that it spread out and gradually **dispersed**. Sometimes it looked white, sometimes blotched and dirty, according to the amount of soil and ashes it carried with it. My uncle's scholarly **acumen** saw at once that it was important enough for a closer inspection, and he ordered a fast boat to be made ready, telling me I could come with him if I wished. I replied that I preferred to go on with my studies, and as it happened he had himself given me some writing to do.

As he was leaving the house he was handed a message from Rectina, wife of **Tascius**, whose house was at the foot of the mountain, so that escape was impossible except by boat. She was terrified by the danger threatening her and **implored** him to rescue her from her fate. He changed his plans, and what he had begun in a spirit of inquiry he completed as a hero. He gave orders for the warships to be launched and went on board himself with the intention of bringing

44

help to many more people besides Rectina, for this lovely stretch of coast was thickly populated. He hurried to the place which everyone else was hastily leaving, steering his course straight for the danger zone. He was entirely fearless, describing each new movement and phase of the **portent** to be noted down exactly as he observed them. Ashes were already falling, hotter and thicker as the ships drew near, followed by bits of **pumice** and blackened stones, charred and cracked by the flames: then suddenly they were in shallow water, and the shore was blocked by the **debris** from the mountain. For a moment my uncle wondered whether to turn back, but when the **helmsman** advised this he refused. . . .

Meanwhile on Mount Vesuvius broad sheets of fire and leaping flames blazed at several points, their bright glare emphasized by the darkness of night. . . . The buildings were now shaking with violent shocks, and seemed to be swaying to and fro as if they were torn from their foundations. Outside on the other hand, there was the danger of falling pumice-stones, even though these were light and **porous**. . . . As a protection against falling objects **they** put pillows on their heads tied down with cloths.

Elsewhere there was daylight by this time, but they were still in darkness, blacker and denser than any night that ever was, which they relieved by lighting torches and various kinds of lamp. My uncle decided to go down to the shore and investigate on the spot the possibility of any escape by sea, but he found the waves still wild and dangerous. . . . Then the flames and smell of sulphur which gave warning of the approaching fire drove the others to take flight. . . . He stood leaning on two slaves and then suddenly collapsed, I imagine because the dense fumes choked his breathing by blocking his windpipe which was **constitutionally** weak and narrow and often inflamed. When daylight returned on the 26th—two days after the last day he had seen—his body was found **intact** and uninjured, still fully

*portent:* sign that a special event is about to happen

*pumice:* lightweight volcanic rock

*debris:* broken pieces of rock

*helmsman:* person who steers the boat

*porous:* full of tiny holes

*they:* Pliny's uncle and the friends he was helping

*constitutionally:* naturally

*intact:* whole

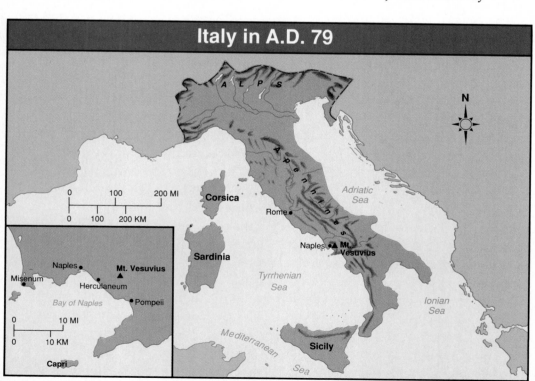

Italy in A.D. 79

Archaeologists have uncovered walls, statues, columns, and mosaics like the one above in the ancient city of Pompeii.

*earth tremors:* small earthquakes

*Campania:* favorite resort area for Romans close to Naples and Mt. Vesuvius

*open space we were in:* the courtyard of their house

*imminent:* likely

*stationary:* standing still

*receded:* moved away

*rent:* split

*Capri:* island in the Bay of Naples

*promontory:* peak of high land

*entreated:* pleaded

clothed and looking more like sleep than death. . . .

\* \* \*

After my uncle's departure I spent the rest of the day with my books, as this was my reason for staying behind. Then I took a bath, dined, and then dozed fitfully for a while. For several days past there had been **earth tremors** which were not particularly alarming because they are frequent in **Campania**: but that night the shocks were so violent that everything felt as if it were not only shaken but overturned. . . .

By now it was dawn, but the light was still dim and faint. The buildings round us were already tottering, and the **open space we were in** was too small for us not to be in real and **imminent** danger if the house collapsed. This finally decided us to leave the town. We were followed by a panic-stricken mob of people . . . who hurried us on our way by pressing hard behind in a dense crowd. Once beyond the

buildings we stopped, and there we had some extraordinary experiences which thoroughly alarmed us. The carriages we had ordered to be brought out began to run in different directions though the ground was quite level, and would not remain **stationary** even when wedged with stones. We also saw the sea sucked away and apparently forced back by the earthquake: at any rate it **receded** from the shore so that quantities of sea creatures were left stranded on dry sand. On the landward side a fearful black cloud was **rent** by forked and quivering bursts of flame, and parted to reveal great tongues of fire, like flashes of lightning magnified in size. . . .

Soon afterwards the cloud sank down to earth and covered the sea; it had already blotted out **Capri** and hidden the **promontory** of Misenum from sight. Then my mother implored, **entreated**, and commanded me to escape as best I could—a young man might escape, whereas she was old and slow and could die in peace as long as she had not been the cause of my death too. I told her I refused to save myself without her, and grasping her hand forced her to quicken her pace. She gave in reluctantly, blaming herself for delaying me. Ashes were already falling, not as yet very thickly. I looked round: a dense black cloud was coming up behind us. . . . "Let us leave the road while we can still see," I said, "or we shall be knocked down and trampled underfoot in the dark by the crowd behind." We had scarcely sat down to rest when darkness fell, not the dark of a moonless or cloudy night, but as if the lamp had been put out in a closed room. You could hear the shrieks of women, the wailing of infants, and the shouting of men; some were calling their parents, others their children or their wives, trying to recognize them by their voices. . . .

A gleam of light returned, but we took this to be a warning of the approaching flames rather than daylight. However, the flames remained some distance off; then darkness came on once more and ashes began to fall again, this time in heavy showers. We rose from time to time and shook them off, otherwise we should have been buried and crushed beneath their weight. . . .

At last the darkness thinned and dispersed into smoke or cloud; then there was genuine daylight, and the sun actually shone out, but yellowish as it is during an eclipse. We were terrified to see everything changed, buried deep in ashes like snowdrifts. We returned to Misenum where we attended to our physical needs as best we could, and then spent an anxious night alternating between hope and fear. . . . But even then, in spite of the dangers we had been through and were still expecting, my mother and I had still no intention of leaving until we had news of my uncle.

In this painting a scribe records Pliny's account of the eruption of Mount Vesuvius. Pliny watched the eruption from his uncle's home about 20 miles from Pompeii.

The eruption of Vesuvius in A.D. 79 buried the town of Pompeii in ash. The town was discovered many centuries later. Since then, archaeologists have removed the ashes and restored most of Pompeii. The town provides valuable information about ancient Roman life. Houses, restaurants, and shops were preserved as they were at the time of the eruption. A bakery in the ancient city even has loaves of bread still inside the ovens.

Reprinted by permission of the Loeb Classical Library from *Pliny the Younger: Letters and Panegyricus*, Vol. I, Betty Radice, translator, Cambridge, Mass.: Harvard University Press, 1969, pp. 427, 429, 431, 433, 441, 443, 445, 447.

# Birthplace of the Olympics

" Here is where the big athletic games of the world started. . . ."

**Jesse Stuart**

The southwestern coast of Greece borders the Ionian Sea. The ancient city of Olympia was built 10 miles inland from the sea.

The ancient Greeks considered Olympia a sacred place. Set in a fertile valley in southern Greece, it was the site of the first Olympic games. The Greeks held the games to honor their gods and their athletes. They also built temples and statues in Olympia. The games are no longer held in Olympia, and the temples and statues are in ruins. But people still travel to visit this ancient place. Writer Jesse Stuart describes his trip to see where the Olympics began.

"Olympia?" I said.

The man in a seat next to me held up two fingers which I interpreted meant we would be there on the second stop. We had been coming up a gradual slope since we left **Pyrgos**. Now we leveled off over a tableland from which we could look back through our broad window at the shining **Ionian Sea**. It was in the distance now. Yet Greeks living here were never out of the sight and sound of the sea. . . .

We went down the valley. "Doesn't look like this land could have been farmed for 2500 years," I said. "Yes, maybe longer."

Then I saw a few houses scattered over the slope of a hill, and I could see hills in all directions except the direction of the valley. Our train was coming to a stop. "Olympia," said the conductor. I wanted to ask:

"Where is the town?" and "Could this be the right place?" Because we were out in the country!

An elderly man met the train and invited us into his hotel and restaurant for lunch. . . . We asked him questions about Olympia and one surprising answer was the town had 750 people living here. This was the area where people had come from all over Greece—from 800 B.C. (and even before) to the present. This was a part of Greece known to the world. . . .

After lunch we walked down the only street which had a few stores on either side. . . . Olympia wasn't as large as our **Greenup, Kentucky** and certainly not as modern. . . .

We walked up to the museum, which we had to see to get the history of the area. . . . At the door a young woman asked me if we needed a

*Pyrgos:* town in southern Greece

*Ionian Sea:* part of the Mediterranean Sea between the southeast coast of Italy and western Greece

*Greenup, Kentucky:* town in northeastern Kentucky

48

guide. "We do," I said. "And you are employed." . . .

She was native Greek and had learned English in Greek schools. She knew . . . much of the history—and when she got off onto Greek mythology, she soared. I had explained to her I wanted to get some pictures of the ruins before the sun went down, and that we had to be on a train at 5:10 P.M., for a seven hour ride back to **Athens**.

Yet we went among the Roman statues. . . .

"How was it so many of these were broken and you couldn't find the pieces?" I asked.

"The Christians did it!" she said.

"We Christians?" I said. "Why?"

"Yes, we Christians," she repeated. "Because we considered all this mythology worship of **pagan** gods."

"Are you sorry we destroyed these?"

"I certainly am."

"So are people over the world."

Olympia had been a religious city for the ancient Greeks. Even when the Romans took over, they worshipped the same pagan gods, mythological gods, only they were under different names so they didn't destroy the statues of pagan gods in Olympia. Our Christian ancestors were the ones who used the sledge hammers and iron bars on some of the world masterpieces of art. And our Christians about 1500 years later were **excavating** this area and putting the pieces together—all that could be found—trying to remake for **posterity** what had been destroyed. . . .

One thing I'd always wanted to see was . . . the entrance to the stadium and the place from which the torch was carried from Olympia to Athens by a relay of runners! This custom still survives and is done today before the Olympics!

*Athens:* capital of Greece

*pagan:* non-Christian

*excavating:* uncovering by digging

*posterity:* future generations

This stone archway led into the great stadium of Olympia where the first Olympic games were held. At first the only Olympic event was a foot race to the end of the stadium.

We walked over the little hill
and down into a valley. . . . Scattered
over a field, with large pines growing
up among them—and meadows of
dandelions and daisies—were the
ruins of a spot made famous by
ancients. What they did here over
two thousand years ago, has been
adopted as a world event today—
the Olympics! . . .

"When did the ancient Olympics
begin, and when did they close?" I
asked our guide.

"The date they began to record
the winners was in 776 B.C.," she said.
"They continued until 393 A.D. They
lasted 1169 years—but actually they
went on longer than this," she said.
"We know they were going on in 884
B.C. Then wars stopped one month
before and one month after the
Olympic races. They stopped the
wars for this big event."

"Oh what a contrast in the world
today," I said quickly. "We stop our
athletic events for wars! Our athletes

have to leave sport games to fight
wars."

"See how high the **bank** is
yonder," she said, pointing to a high
bank by the river. "You can see how
much dirt was removed. . . . The
Germans did this from 1875-1881.
They used 300 men here for six years
to excavate Olympia!". . .

"I told you the statues were first
destroyed by the Christians," she
said. "But the Christians had help.
What the big earthquake didn't
destroy in 532 A.D., the second one
finished in 551. The earthquakes
tumbled the temples. You will see
when we go among them." Our lady
guide explained the streets to us.
Where many columns were still
standing was the **Palaistra**. There
was a circular foundation of stones
with large stones lying near. This
was the small temple finished by
**Alexander the Great** for his father,
**Phillip of Macedonia**. This one was
erected in 338 B.C. . . .

*Palaistra:* public
place for exercise
and training;
a gymnasium

*Alexander the
Great:* ruler and
conqueror of a
vast empire that
included Greece

*Phillip of
Macedonia:* (Philip)
king of Macedonia,
an area north of
Greece. Philip
conquered nearly
all of Greece.

The great stone temples and buildings of Olympia were gradually covered with soil by
earthquakes and landslides. Archaeologists began uncovering the ruins in the 1820s.

"Now, here is something I want you to see," our guide said. Down in an excavation, ten feet or more below the ground surface on which the ancients walked, was another level on which still more ancient people had walked. Here lay **unhewn** stones in squares, oblongs, and circles. "This is prehistoric," she said. "Olympia was built upon the site of another temple. We know this dates back to 1650 B.C. —maybe much earlier."

"Who were the people here then?" I asked.

"Maybe the **Peliasgians**," she replied. "We do not know. Nor do we know the people here before them." . . .

Now, we were within a few yards of the entrance to the stadium. On our way, we had passed under what was believed to be an old Roman **aqueduct**. . . .

"Here is what you have been wanting to see," she said. "And there is sun enough for you to get pictures."

"Well, this surprises me," I said. "I expected it to be larger."

"It's larger than you think," she told us. "About 45,000 people could watch the events!" . . .

Here is where the big athletic games of the world started, I thought, as I climbed upon the bank to take pictures of the field. I wanted to send them back to basketball and football coaches I knew in Kentucky who had

Runners in ancient Greece carried a torch from Olympia to Athens. Today runners still carry the torch from Olympia to the place where the Olympic games are held.

talked about this spot of earth and who wanted to come here and who had planned to come someday.

After staying here as long as we could, for we knew Greek trains didn't wait, we walked . . . slowly back toward the station. . . . It had been a race for us to get here, but we made it.

*unhewn:* uncut

*Peliasgians:* (Pelasgians) the earliest inhabitants of Greece and the surrounding area

*aqueduct:* elevated structure built to support pipe that carried water

The Roman Emperor Theodosius ended the Olympic games in A.D. 394 because the athletes were interested only in winning money, not in honor. No Olympic games were held for 1,500 years. The games were started again in 1896 to promote world peace. About 13 nations and 285 athletes competed that year in Athens, Greece. Today the Olympics are held every four years in a different country. In 1976 Olympia became a national park. The land there is planted with olive trees just as it was during the time of the ancient Olympics.

From Jesse Stuart, *Dandelion on the Acropolis* (Lynnville, Tenn.: Archer Editions Press, 1978), pp. 111–17. Reprinted by permission.

# EASTERN EUROPE AND THE SOVIET UNION

*taiga:* subarctic region with many spruce and fir trees

*steppes:* dry flatlands

*tundra:* arctic and subarctic region with frozen subsoil that supports only dwarf plants

*ethnic groups:* people who share common customs, language, or history

Imagine a land where the sun never sets, a land so wide from east to west that when it is day at one end it is still night at the other. There is such a land—the Soviet Union—the largest country in the world. Symbolized by a large black bear, the Soviet Union has one foot firmly planted in Europe and the other in Asia.

Spreading across this wide region are landforms of seemingly endless variety. Here is the **taiga**, the largest forest area in the world; the fertile grass-covered plains of the **steppes**; and the cold and treeless flatlands of the **tundra**. Here are the burning black sands of the Kara Kum desert, in the southwest, where the temperature can rise above 120 degrees Fahrenheit, and the breathtaking cold and permanently frozen ground of Siberia. The people of the Soviet Union are as varied as the land. Some 90 different **ethnic groups** speak their own languages and use four different alphabets.

The Soviets are a determined people. Ruled for almost 500 years by stronghanded leaders known as tsars, most of the people made their living from the land. Before the 1800s, they lived in what many Western Europeans considered a "backward" farming country. By 1900, Soviet industry was thriving, overshadowing agriculture. At the end of World War II, the Soviet Union was the strongest country in Europe and Asia, a superpower that rivaled the United States.

After the war, the Soviets spread their power and established communist governments throughout neighboring Eastern Europe. But Eastern Europe had a rich history before it came under Soviet control. Although most of the eight countries—Albania, Bulgaria, Romania,

Hungary, Yugoslavia, Czechoslovakia, East Germany, and Poland—took their present boundaries less than 100 years ago, people have lived in Eastern Europe for at least 200,000 years.

Over the centuries, the landscape has shaped the daily life of the people of Eastern Europe. Broad mountain ranges shelter towns and fields. The fertile soil of the plains provides the people with much of the food they eat. Cargo travels up and down the many rivers that crisscross the region. These rivers provide water for crops and for electrical power. In the past, much of the region was rural, and most of the people worked the land. Farming—raising crops and livestock—was the main source of income. Now there are many cities, and industry has grown.

Eastern Europe is a quilt of cultures. Slavs, Germans, Slovaks, Czechs, Turks, and Gypsies, and dozens of other cultural groups make their home in these eight countries. Though most people do not have access to a large variety of groceries and manufactured products, not every Eastern European country has the same standard of living. And each is at a different stage of economic development. Today the countries of Eastern Europe are striving to cast off the cloak of Soviet influence and are beginning to take steps toward this goal.

The people of Siberia have learned to adapt to the cold winters. Fur-lined clothing protects them from the icy winds, and they use sleds to travel across ice and snow.

This unit includes the accounts of writers who have visited the Soviet Union and Eastern Europe.

■ Jon Humboldt Gates tells of his trip through **Moscow** and its surrounding area. He describes the warm and friendly people he met.

☐ Stan Grossfeld takes us to coldest **Siberia**. He tells about life at minus 50° Fahrenheit in the city of Yakutsk.

■ Brian Hall traveled across Romania, Bulgaria, and Hungary. He describes the way of life in a small village in **Hungary**.

# A Tour of the Soviet Union

❝ I'm sorry," he apologized, "but there are no highway maps. We are all out.❞

**Jon Humboldt Gates**

Moscow is the capital of and largest city in the Soviet Union. It is the center of Soviet politics, industry, and culture.

*Trans Siberian Express:* railroad that crosses the Soviet Union

*mega-city:* very large, super-city

*epicenter:* center of everything

*Kremlin:* ancient walled fortress that is now the center of Soviet government

*bureaucrats:* government officials

*Spasskaya Tower:* a Kremlin building

*Red Square:* large open area outside the Kremlin

*itinerary:* outline for a trip

*Lada:* small economy car

*Intourist:* Soviet travel agency

For many years travel in the Soviet Union was discouraged by the government. This changed when Mikhail Gorbachev became the Soviet leader in 1985. Under Gorbachev's new policies, people were allowed to move more freely around this huge country. People from other countries could also visit the Soviet Union more easily. Jon Gates, an American writer, traveled the cities and back roads of the Soviet Union in the 1980s. ∽

Arriving in Moscow aboard the **Trans Siberian Express** had been like stepping out of a time machine. The Soviet **mega-city** shocked me. Streets wide enough to land jumbo jets, pedestrians striding at a New York City pace, subway stations that looked like fine art museums, and at the **epicenter** stood the **Kremlin**. Limousines of military men and **bureaucrats** popped in and out of **Spasskaya Tower** on **Red Square**.

My pre-planned **itinerary** would route me through the Soviet capital several times. All the highways of the region pointed toward Moscow as if it were the ancient hub of a great spoked wheel. The city itself was circled by five highways that formed a series of rings from the Kremlin out to the suburbs.

It had taken me half the day just to get to the eastern edge of

Moscow. Early in the morning, I rented a little Soviet-built **Lada**. Getting the car hadn't been a problem, just a few signatures and an American passport. A friendly **Intourist** agent smiled and held the keys out to me.

"Have a very good time. We will see you in two weeks."

"What about a map?"

"I'm sorry," he apologized, "but there are no highway maps. We are all out."

I drove away from the hotel in disbelief, nosing the Lada into the rush of Moscow traffic. After [I had driven] two hours on the wrong road, a policeman pulled me over and pointed me back toward Moscow. The patient, older man listened to my story, but offered only a sympathetic nod and pointed over the trees toward Southern Russia or the Indian

Ocean, somewhere far over the horizon. . . .

Fifteen minutes later, the four-lane highway tapered into a narrow, two-way road **traversing** fields and colorful country villages. Every home had a TV antenna and an out-house. People carried well water in buckets.

Scores of big trucks rumbled along the asphalt pavement, spewing black smoke out their stacks and holding back lines of darting passenger cars. The traffic was thick. . . .

After . . . an hour and a half, the road crossed a small river bending through a grove of birch trees where an outdoor grill and picnic area had attracted a crowd of motorists. . . .

Two women in white aprons passively tended the grill in a grassy meadow alongside the highway. My taste buds blossomed at the skewers of beef and onion **shashleeks** barbecuing over a bed of hot coals. The older woman in white scraped the skewered meat and onions onto a paper plate and weighed it in grams on a scale. She used an **abacus** to figure the cost. . . .

After lunch . . . I lay back in the grass and closed my eyes. The high-way sounds **receded**. . . .

\* \* \* \*

The road sign pointed north to **Suzdal**. I was surprised to see a dozen people hitchhiking wearing business suits or dresses. A few carried briefcases. It was 5:30 in the afternoon, on the northern edge of Vladimir, an industrial urban center 120 miles east of Moscow.

I swerved over and **magnetized** six potential riders.

"Suzdal!" I yelled out the window.

Immediately, all three doors opened, and the car filled with people and briefcases. I pulled away slowly. The small Soviet **compact** lost its pep with the extra seven hundred pounds aboard.

*traversing:* crossing

*shashleeks:* pieces of meat and vegetables cooked on skewers (sticks)

*abacus:* device with sliding pieces on rods that is used for counting

*receded:* faded away

*Suzdal:* small city north of Moscow

*magnetized:* pulled in; attracted

*compact:* small economy car

Moscow's wide boulevards become small two-lane roads as they stretch into the countryside. The historic town of Zagorsk is 40 miles outside the capital.

*abruptly:* suddenly

The city of Vladimir ended **abruptly** at a row of tall trees lining an irrigation ditch. Across the ditch, farmland spread into the distance.

I scanned all the new faces. They were a cheery group. ''Thank God it's Friday'' seemed to generate universal relief.

''I speak English very well,'' a heavily accented voice said from the back seat. Surprised, I glanced in my rearview mirror, then turned for a quick acknowledgement to the man in the middle who spoke. His wide smile supported a pair of thick, dark-rimmed glasses and a small wool sporting cap.

''That's great,'' I said. ''I haven't met many Russians who speak English. Did you study at the University?''

''I speak English very well,'' he repeated. Everyone in the car snickered.

''Hmmm, I see. So you don't really speak English. You can't understand me. Right?'' Another pause.

*thumbed:* held out a thumb to ask for a ride; hitchhiked

*U.S.S.R.:* Union of Soviet Socialist Republics, complete name of the Soviet Union

*Charlie Chaplin:* silent film actor and comedian of the 1920s

*ruble:* Soviet money, similar to a U.S. dollar bill

Few people have cars in the rural areas of the Soviet Union. They walk, hitchhike, or rely on trains and buses to travel long distances.

''Thank you very much,'' he laughed. ''I speak English very well, ha ha ha.''

We sailed along at 60 miles an hour surrounded by a sprawling sea of chocolate-dark soil, lush green field crops and a huge blue sky. Two tractors rambled along the horizon. A few billboards and it would look like the American Midwest. The Russian jibber jabber in the back seat made me feel relaxed. . . .

When I rented the car that morning, I didn't realize that I would be ferrying hitchhikers across Russian highways, or that hitchhiking was an acceptable form of Soviet transportation. I'd **thumbed** across the States a few times, but it seemed different in the **U.S.S.R.**

My first riders that day had been a young boy and his grandmother. She drew a map to her country home in case I wanted to stop for tea on my way back to Moscow. Then a stocky middle-aged truck driver climbed into the passenger seat, sporting a **Charlie Chaplin** moustache and a tweed suit. A small brown felt hat perched on his head as if it would only be there a minute.

And now I had a carload of Vladimir commuters. The hitchhiker in the front seat pulled out a one **ruble** bill.

''For gasoline.''

I tried not to accept the money, but two more rubles came from the back seat.

''I have coupons for gas,'' I bargained, taking them from my shirt pocket and holding them up for proof. I waved coupons. My passengers waved rubles.

It was four against one. They insisted I take the gas money. ''If not for gasoline, then we are buying your dinner for you.'' End of discussion.

Suzdal broke the northern landscape with a fairytale skyline of

Gold stars cover the blue onion domes of a Suzdal cathedral built in the 1200s. The Archbishop's Palace on the right is now a museum of history and art.

old world Russian architecture. Scores of **bulbous onion domes** dotted the **turreted** walls of monasteries and churches. The center dome of Suzdal's **Kremlin billowed** like a midnight blue hot air balloon drawn to a point. Golden stars and gilded orthodox crosses adorned the historic crown. The **Kamenka River** flowed through the town.

I dropped my passengers off in a **quaint** residential area of ornate wooden homes and narrow streets. Only a few thousand people lived in Suzdal.

When the comedian got out, he bent over and looked back inside the car with a grin on his face. "Thank you very much. I speak English very well. Good-bye."

The standard of living in Moscow and Suzdal is slowly improving. But even in the Soviet Union's western region, the center of power and industry, basic goods are still in short supply. Standing in line to buy items such as meat or shoes is a way of life. The waiting list for a car still can be five years long. Some economists think that recent moves toward **capitalism** will help reduce these shortages.

*bulbous onion domes:* refers to an old Russian building style in which roofs had a round shape, pointed at the top

*turreted:* having small towers

*Kremlin:* the fortress or stronghold of a Russian city

*billowed:* swelled, expanded

*Kamenka River:* small river north of Moscow

*quaint :* old-fashioned

*capitalism:* economic system in which business and industry are controlled by individuals

From Jon Humboldt Gates, *Soviet Passage* (Eureka, Calif.: Summer Run Publishing, 1988), pp. 69–73, 78–82. Reprinted by permission.

# Winter in Siberia

" . . . it's very hard to walk fast, there's a shortage of oxygen, and it hurts to breathe."

**Stan Grossfeld**

Sleds are a popular form of transportation in Yakutsk. In January the average temperature is 60 degrees below zero.

Siberia is a vast region in the northern and eastern Soviet Union. It covers half the area of the Soviet Union but has only one eighth of its population. Many factories are in Siberia because it is rich in natural resources such as coal and oil. But snow and ice cover much of the region. Stan Grossfeld traveled across Siberia in 1987 and tells about life at minus 50 degrees Fahrenheit. ∞

*Yakutsk, March 16*

Half of the Soviet Union is covered by permafrost—permanently frozen ground. Since 1943 the Soviets have built their houses on stilts sunk into the ground. **Prior to** that, when the top few feet thawed out in the summer, houses sank. All heating systems are above ground so as not to melt the permafrost.

"In winter we practically don't see the sun, not only because daytime is short but because of the **habitation fog**, which starts appearing at minus 40 degrees **F** and covers Yakutsk like a big hat," said one of my local **escorts**. Habitation fog is formed by the **exhalations** of both man and machine. This frozen "people mist" hovers over villages like an **eerie blue funk**. It causes accidents and flight cancellations. . . .

"When the temperature hits **56** [minus 68.8 degrees F] all classes up to the seventh grade are cancelled. All children are happy because they can play hockey. But it's very hard to walk fast, there's a shortage of oxygen, and it hurts to breathe." . . .

"Here we get two seasons. Summer in June, July, and half of August. You must come back in summer; the mosquitoes love the blood of foreigners."

He laughs, then continues. "Then it snows. The first snow always melts, and then the leaves turn yellow. In one week winter comes."

The Hotel Lena has a **decompression-chamber** system to get into the lobby. You have to go through three doors to shake the cold. . . .

Let's talk cold. At 6:15 A.M. I emerge from . . . the Sunny Hotel and walk through the three doors of doom into minus 49 degrees F. Breath number one: The nose hairs freeze

*prior to:* before

*habitation fog:* fog caused by human activities

*F:* Fahrenheit

*escorts:* guides

*exhalations:* breath or vapor

*eerie blue funk:* strange blue fog

*56:* minus 56 degrees Celsius

*decompression-chamber:* place for going from level to level gradually

together. Exhale: The nose hairs thaw out. Within ten minutes the fingers ache despite three layers of gloves. Silk first, then wool, then **polypropylene**. . . .

Five hundred trucks bring coal from **Magadan** on the Sea of Okhotsk, 620 miles away. The road is icy, dark, and treacherous. . . .

The trucks, specially made in Czechoslovakia, always travel in pairs, and the hoods of their engines are wrapped in quilted fabric. Once, when the temperature hit minus 76 degrees F, 150 trucks were stranded on the road to Magadan, their rubber tires split by cold. . . .

To imagine how cold it is, drink an icy **frappe** very quickly and imagine that aching pain in your head stretching all the way down to your toes. . . .

Back inside the three doors of the Sunny Hotel, the woman behind the desk has a coat draped around her shoulders. She looks like a deep-sea diver trying to stay dry in leaky chambers.

In my **suite** the black cameras turn white. I try going back to bed with clothes and covers piled on. Still not enough warmth. So I write from the bathtub, where the hot water pipes are.

*polypropylene:* type of plastic that holds warmth and does not crack in extreme cold

*Magadan:* seaport and industrial city in Siberia southeast of Yakutsk

*frappe:* (frappé) partially frozen beverage

*suite:* hotel room arranged like an apartment

**Average January Temperatures in the Soviet Union**

ARCTIC OCEAN

Bering Sea

Baltic Sea

Moscow

Black Sea

Caspian Sea

Aral Sea

Yakutsk

Sea of Okhotsk

N

0     500     1000 MI

0     500     1000 KM

Above 32°F
32° to 0°F
0° to -30°F
Below -30°F

The harsh climate of Siberia makes it very difficult to use the region's rich natural resources. Modern machines have made it possible to build roads and drill oil. But the icy cold of winter and the wet mud of summer make all work difficult. Few Soviets care to live under such conditions. Still Siberia continues to be developed. The need for resources demands that the climate be overcome.

Text reprinted with permission from *The Whisper of Stars: A Siberian Journey*, pp. 115, 118, 130, by Stan Grossfeld, Copyright © 1987, 1988, $24.95 cloth, published by The Globe Pequot Press, Chester, CT 06412.

# Village Life in Hungary

" People have food now, and clothes, and even a car. . . . What else could they want? "

**Brian Hall**

Budapest is the only large city in Hungary. The capital city is home to one-fifth of Hungary's 10.5 million people.

*Zsóka:* a Hungarian woman who works in a book company and is a friend of the author

*Ági:* friend of Zsóka who works as a hospital researcher

*forints:* Hungarian money

*Budapest:* capital city of Hungary

*kilo:* kilogram, or about 2.2 pounds

*affordability:* amount people are able to pay

*daunting:* discouraging

*Trabant:* small economy car made in East Germany

*Győr:* city in northwestern Hungary

*ruefully:* with sorrow or pity

**H**ungary is a small country in Eastern Europe. It was under the control of a communist government from the end of World War II until 1990. During that time it became more industrialized and less agricultural. In the 1980s Hungary began moving closer to democracy and capitalism. Brian Hall describes the life of one family in a small Hungarian village in 1983. ∽

"The people in the villages live very well," **Zsóka** says. . . . "Much better than we in the city." . . .

"Oh yes," [**Ági**] says happily. "They *are* rich. But they work seven days a week."

Zsóka works only five days a week. Her salary is pretty average: 5,100 **forints**, or about $130, a month. With extra work . . . in the evenings, she raises that to about $170. (A private doctor in **Budapest** can make twelve times that amount.) The basic necessities are cheap. Zsóka's rent is $16 a month. A **kilo** of bread costs 15 cents. A bus ride is 4 cents. But as one moves away from this most basic level, **affordability** drops rapidly. A pound of meat or cheese costs a dollar. A pair of shoes, $20 to $25. A dress, $30; a suit, $60. For anything that is not food or clothing, the prices are **daunting**. Zsóka's black-and-white television set cost her nearly a

month's salary. A **Trabant**, the cheapest car available, would cost her more than a year's salary. A small house, over a decade's salary. Worst of all, she would need the money all at once: it is impossible to buy on credit in Hungary. . . .

At the station in **Győr**, we are met by Ági's brother Béla. . . . He escorts us out to a new beige Trabant. "My family just bought it," he says, proudly patting the plastic hood. "The waiting list for these is five years long now." . . .

We all squeeze in, and the little Trabant blubbers into life. At the first hill, the poor thing whines and slows to a crawl. "Hungary is a small country," Béla says to me **ruefully**. "We don't need very fast cars."

The sun is going down when we arrive at the village near Győr in which Ági's and Béla's parents live. Chain-link fences line the dirt streets;

**60**

behind them stand solid stone houses. The parents (a stout, strong peasant mother and a smaller, frailer father) come out and kiss each of us on both cheeks. I forget my Hungarian, and instead of saying "Good evening," I say "Good night," and everyone laughs. Ági bounds delightedly into the house.

The mother is named Margit, and the father, György. They live in a typical village house—square, single-storied, under a **pyramidal** roof of tiles. There is a large cluttered kitchen, a smaller, cluttered dining room, two bedrooms, and a cramped, **ambiguous** space piled nearly to the ceiling with bedding. Both bedrooms and the dining room are filled with solid, dark, wooden furniture. Hangings, photographs, clocks, and curtains cover most of the wall space. The beds are immense, the bloated mattresses swelling in the middle like pitcher's mounds. A television set babbles at the end of the master bed, and Ági's father returns to it as soon as the introductions are over.

The house sits on about a quarter-acre lot. Built onto the back is a garage filled with agricultural tools. Sticking out from the garage is the stable, where the cow is kept. Next to the stable is the chicken coop, and behind the chicken coop is the pigpen. Between coop, stable, and pen—everywhere, in fact, except where the driveway is—lies the garden, which, since it is mid-March, is beginning to show sprouts of the earliest vegetables. **Trellises** for grapevines have been put up wherever they do not block sunlight from the garden— over the chicken coop, above the stone paving that skirts the stable, across the driveway. The whole lot is enclosed by fruit trees, which stand on all four sides. . . .

The family also owns a plot of land that lies just outside the village,

about fifty yards away. Ági takes us there. The plot is not large—something around an acre—but every square foot of it is used. Half has been prepared for grain; the other half is an apple-tree nursery. Ági explains that the tree nursery is unusual, the result of a daring decision by her father. As the produce market frees up, more and more villagers are making use of whatever land they have. For borders and small pieces of unused land, apple trees are popular, because they bear heavily and are fairly hardy; but people don't want to start from seed, so they buy her father's young trees. . . .

Through a screen of beeches, we can see a very large field. In the distance, a tractor charges like a bull, head down, flipping the soil. Ági

*pyramidal:* shaped with four triangular sides meeting in a point at the top

*ambiguous:* not clearly defined

Horse-drawn carts and rows of tile-roofed houses are common sights in Hungary's small rural villages.

*trellises:* wooden frames

says that her family owned part of the field until the fifties, but that the whole thing now is a **cooperative**. Her father used to work in the cooperative, spending evenings and weekends on his own plot, but he retired from it two years ago. Now he is weakening, and Ági's mother does most of the work with the garden, the grain, and the young trees, while her father feeds the animals and trains the vines.

By the time we return to the house, dinner is ready, and the economics of this rich village life begin to be apparent. Baskets on the table hold bread that was made from wheat grown in the family plot. The wine in the bottles comes from the grapes that grew last year above the driveway. The two pig's feet in the big pot of broth **originated** in the pen behind the chicken coop. The chicken comes from the coop itself. The cheese and sour-cream sauce for the chicken come from the cow in the stable. The peppers and tomatoes in the pickled salad were grown in the garden

behind the pigpen. The sliced apples were picked last November from the trees by the front gate. The yoghurt for dessert also came from the cow, and the strawberries in the preserves in the yoghurt came from the garden next to the chicken coop. . . . The food in the stores in Budapest, especially the bread and preserves, is nothing like this.

Ági's mother never sits down, as she is kept busy bringing platters in and taking empty dishes out. Now and then she relaxes long enough to nibble, standing, on a **pig crackling** that she fishes out of a big metal bowl on the china chest. Béla complains to his mother about the broth, and then about the sauce, and although I met him only hours ago, I can barely restrain myself from kicking him under the table. . . .

Later, Ági, Zsóka, and I take a walk around the village's poorly lit streets. Ági tells us that her mother makes most of her own and her husband's clothes. The curtains and the tower of bedding in the ambiguous

Hungary's countryside is a patchwork of small farms. Hungary exports many food crops including wheat, corn, sugar beets, wine, and livestock.

Fresh produce is piled high in the stalls of Budapest's Tolbuhin Market. Budapest relies on farmers in rural areas for its supply of produce.

space were also made by her mother. Moreover, only a fraction of what her parents grow is consumed at home. Much produce from the garden ends up at the market in Budapest. Her father also rents out their machinery to other families in the village, and sometimes, in the spring, they sell piglets, or a calf, if they haven't enough grass to raise it themselves. With the money they have saved up, Ági's parents bought the apartment that Béla is now living in. Just

recently, they paid for the Trabant. Ági views her family as evidence that things are getting better. People have food now, and clothes, and even a car to drive on Sundays. What else could they want?

"And there is nothing unusual about my family," Ági says. "Many of the families in this village are doing just as well." In the darkness beyond the feeble lamplight, I can see other well-kept houses, other trellises, other chicken coops.

Brian Hall traveled by bicycle in Eastern Europe. In Hungary he pedaled past many prosperous farms. Most farmers in Hungary live on **collective farms.** But many people, like Ági's family, have their own gardens or small fields where they grow produce to sell on their own. Agriculture in Hungary is very success- ful. Farm products make up a quarter of the nation's exports. And people in Hungary have the best choice of foods in Eastern Europe. In 1989 the new democratic government in Hungary declared it would set up a **market economy.**

*collective farms:* farms where groups of families own the land and share profits

*market economy:* system in which people can buy and sell goods freely, without government control

Excerpts from *Stealing From a Deep Place*, pp. 255–59, by Brian Hall. Copyright © 1988 by Brian Hall. Reprinted by permission of Hill & Wang, a division of Farrar, Straus, and Giroux, Inc.

## UNIT 5

# NORTH AFRICA AND THE MIDDLE EAST

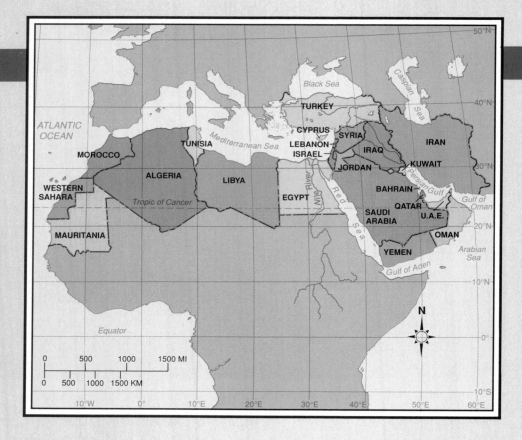

*oases:* (plural of *oasis*) fertile land in the middle of the desert

**I**n the southern interior of the Arabian Peninsula, in the oil-rich country of Saudi Arabia, there is a place where the trackless, shifting sand dunes rise high into the air and seem to grab the sky. For hundreds of square miles there is nothing but salt basins and dry, choking sand. This place has a name—Rub al Khalir. It is one of the largest sand deserts in the world. It is the Empty Quarter, where no one lives and nothing grows. There is no water here, and water means life, especially in North Africa and the Middle East.

In the Middle East, it is the mountains that keep the water away. Bounding the land, they block the path of the rain-laden clouds and force them to release their precious drops of water before the water can reach the interior lands.

But water does flow in some parts of the Middle East and North Africa. Where there are springs and rivers, date palms and grains can grow. **Oases** are lush and valleys are emerald green. Indeed, the Nile Valley and the Fertile Crescent, watered by the Tigris and Euphrates rivers, were both cradles of civilization.

Where the water was, the people settled, grew crops, and built cities, cities that still stand today, sun-soaked and sprawling. On the Nile, there is colorful, bustling Cairo; on the Tigris, the once-splendid and mysterious Baghdad; on the Mediterranean, war-torn Beirut. And linking the continents of Europe and Asia, at the mouth of the Black Sea, is Istanbul. In bygone times, it had other names—Byzantium, Constantinople. For more that 2,000 years it has thrived, a bridge for overland and sea traffic between the East and the West.

Most of the people of North Africa and the Middle East, though, do not live in the cities. Instead they live on and work the land. Many, like the Egyptian *fellahin*, farm rented land using hand tools that have changed little in 6,000 years. Other, like the Israelis of the farming settlements known as *kibbutzim*, use modern equipment. They share their labor and the produce of the desert land they have made bloom. Still others, like the desert-dwelling Bedouins, carry on the old nomadic life of their ancestors. Secure in their beliefs and traditions, they live as they have for centuries, moving from oasis to oasis, tending herds of sheep or goats or camels.

The people of these two regions are a study in contrasts, between city dweller and farmer, between the oil rich and the hungry poor. They are also a study in conflict. In their own minds the people are Arabs, Iranians, Turks, Israelis, Palestinians, Armenians, or Kurds. These groups have not always lived together peacefully. But to the rest of the world they are all a part of an ancient land steeped in history and tradition, a land where one of the earliest western civilizations began, a land that gave birth to three of the world's great religions—Judaism, Christianity, and Islam.

Most of the people who live in North Africa and the Middle East practice the religion of Islam. Many Muslim women wear veils and long, loosely fitted robes in public.

This unit describes modern life in three countries in North Africa and the Middle East.

- In a book about her experiences in Jerusalem, **Israel**, journalist Grace Halsell discusses Jewish and Islamic beliefs.
- In her autobiography, Jehan Sadat remembers celebrating a special holiday while growing up in **Egypt**.
- Writer Alison R. Lanier explains customs and gives advice to business people who visit **Saudi Arabia**.

# Journey to Jerusalem

" If I saw mineral matter, old Hassan, looking at the rock, sees eternity. "

**Grace Halsell**

The ancient shrines and temples of Jerusalem are sacred to members of the Jewish, Islamic, and Christian faiths.

*United Nations:* organization formed in 1945 to promote world peace

*socialists:* people who believe land and goods should not be owned privately

*orthodox:* following the old ways

*secular:* not religious

*Yemenite Jews:* Jews originally from Yemen in Arabia

*celestial:* heavenly

*prophesy:* (prophecy) prediction

*mystic aura:* sense of mystery

*synagogue:* building used by Jews for worship and religious study

*niche:* nook

**B**oth Muslims and Jews have lived in the land called Palestine for centuries. Palestine is an area in the Middle East that was made up of Israel and part of Jordan. Between 600 and 1800 Arabs controlled most of this area. The Jews who once lived there scattered to other countries. Thousands returned, starting in the late 1800s. In 1948 the **United Nations** set up a separate Jewish nation called Israel. As more Jews came to the new country, conflict between Arabs and Jews increased. Writer Grace Halsell describes her life among Jews and Muslims in Israel today. ෴

*Going to the Synagogues*

In 1948, Israel became a Jewish state, founded largely by practicing **socialists** who were nonpracticing Jews. "Most of Israel's independence heroes," explains one **orthodox** rabbi, "were people who deeply valued Jewish tradition but also wanted to build a fundamentally **secular** state—where religion would have a respected place on the sidelines." . . .

David Ben-Gurion, Israel's first prime minister, wanted to round up the Jews from all corners of the earth and bring them "home" to Palestine, and so he said to the **Yemenite Jews**, "Come home to Israel." They did not know it was a place on a map. Israel, Zion, Jerusalem—all were names for some **celestial** paradise. They thought

it was **prophesy** that wings were provided to get them there.

The United States Air Force cooperated by providing waves of "magic carpets"—transporting sixty-five thousand Yemenite Jews from their desert homes to Israel. Flight crews recall how amazed they were to find the Yemenites camping in the aisles, lighting fires to brew their tea. Even aboard the plane, they carried on their desert way of life, setting up portable altars, tending to their children and animals. An ancient, **mystic aura** seemed to surround them.

This ancient mystic aura prevails in a "living museum" or Yemenite **synagogue**. . . .

On entering the synagogue's small **niche** for women, I step in front of four old women, very wrinkled, and ease myself alongside three very young women, none yet twenty. . . . One old woman is saying—so I am able to gather from her gestures—that I should have a kerchief over my head, and the young women are saying, oh, let her alone. We all peer from time to time into the main hall to see what the men are doing, as the women must follow their lead as to when to sit or stand and what prayers to say or sing. . . .

I also went to a **Persian** synagogue, whose members are descendants of the Jewish community in a town in Persia where they had been influenced by Muslim culture. The Jews thus introduced into their synagogues a number of decorations, services, and ceremonies identical to those in the **mosques**. . . . A few of these Persian Jews retain a double first name—Jewish and Muslim. One finds names such as Abraham Abdualla Cohen. . . .

Since almost all the Jews in the United States are **Ashkenazim**, and

I had previously attended only Ashkenazic synagogues, it was perhaps only natural that when I went to a Jerusalem Ashkenazic synagogue I would feel at home. Again, I climb up to a loft that separates the women from the men. I immediately notice the blond hair and blue eyes of several of the women around me. Also I hear Western music with which I can easily identify. There is a curtain over a **lattice window** that separates us from the men, but the curtain has been tossed over the top of the lattice so that I can see the men in the main hall better than in the other synagogues. . . .

My interest in various synagogues led me to meet an Israeli, Joseph Hayardeni, forty-eight, who is a schoolteacher by profession but whose passion is his religion and its meaning to his nation. . . .

He repeats his strong conviction that Jews, to retain their religion, must believe every word of their Holy Scripture. ". . . God will allow us to live here only if we are faithful

*Persian:* of Persia, the former name of Iran

*mosques:* Muslim holy temples

*Ashkenazim:* Jews who settled in middle and northern Europe

*lattice window:* window screened by crossed wood or metal strips

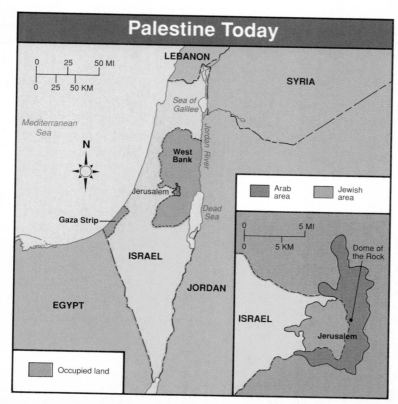

**Palestine Today**

LEBANON

SYRIA

Sea of Galilee

Jordan River

Mediterranean Sea

N

West Bank

Jerusalem

Dead Sea

Gaza Strip

Arab area    Jewish area

ISRAEL

JORDAN

EGYPT

ISRAEL

Dome of the Rock

Jerusalem

Occupied land

The gold-capped Dome of the Rock is a holy place for Muslims, Christians, and Jews. Muslims believe that Mohammed ascended to heaven from the rock housed in this shrine.

*dispersed:* sent to different places

*strife:* trouble; difficulty

*Mahmud ali Hassan:* Arab who restored Arabian art objects

*mosaics:* pictures and designs made of bits of stone or glass

*shards:* pieces of broken pottery

*Dome of the Rock:* holy shrine in Jerusalem

*revere:* show great respect for

*edifices:* buildings

*antedates:* comes before

*Abraham:* ancestor of the Jews and Muslims

to the Jewish religion and, if we lose our Judaism, we have no right to Israel." As for the Palestinian Arabs who were **dispersed** in 1948, "Jews would like to welcome them to return—but then we would become a minority, and if we are a minority, we are nothing. And we waited two thousand years to return to our land." He sees endless **strife**.

*The Old Walled City*

**Mahmud ali Hassan** . . . is a sculptor, a restorer of **mosaics** and **shards**, an archaeologist. . . .

One day, early in our friendship, Hassan and I visited the magnificent **Dome of the Rock**. . . .

At the entrance to the Dome of the Rock, Hassan and I, along with dozens of other visitors from around the world, removed our shoes and, once inside, walked on ancient, richly textured Oriental rugs. After a half-dozen steps we reached a guardrail that framed a large boulder. I was startled by the unexpected dimensions of the rock.

We stood silently. I saw a large mass of stone, mineral matter from the earth's crust, a boulder like other boulders I have seen in countless regions of the earth. The rock, which rises above the ground to my shoulders and covers an area half the size of a tennis court, dominates the entire space within the shrine. Visitors come here not specifically to pray, but to admire and **revere** the rock. This shrine—the most beautiful in Jerusalem and one of the most beautiful religious **edifices** in the world—was built for one sole purpose: to protect and enhance the huge rock.

If I saw mineral matter, old Hassan, looking at the rock, sees eternity. The rock, he believes, is the foundation stone of the universe. "It marks the center of the world," he told me. And the center of his faith. The holy stone, Hassan believes, **antedates** the three great religions, Judaism, Christianity, and Islam. . . .

"Muslims and Christians as well as Jews connect this great rock with **Abraham**," Hassan continued. "He

**68**

began his journey to this rock in **Mesopotamia** between the **Tigris and Euphrates rivers**, a part of modern Iraq. He walked to what is now Turkey and later traveled to the Judean highlands of Jordan. Eventually, at this rock, he prepared, as a sign of his love of God, to sacrifice his son Isaac, but God **stayed** Abraham's hand.

"**Muhammad** tells us Abraham was the actual founder of our Islamic religion," Hassan continued. "Our quarrel has never been with Jews as Jews or with the great religion of Judaism. The places that the Jews and Christians revere as holy, we revere as holy. The prophets the Jews and Christians revere as holy, we revere

as holy. My holy book the Koran is filled with **devout** references to Noah, Abraham, Moses, and Christ. As for this great rock," Hassan concluded, "Muhammad believed it had its origins in Paradise. And it was from this sacred rock that Muhammad was transported by God to heaven.". . .

After Christianity, Hassan's religion is the world's second religion. Every fifth person in the world is a Muslim. The Muslims live in forty nations, including Egypt, Turkey, Iraq, Iran, Afghanistan, Saudi Arabia, and Libya. And until 1948, and the creation of Israel within old Palestine, Islam was the dominant faith in what we call the Holy Land.

*Mesopotamia:* ancient name of land now part of Iraq

*Tigris and Euphrates rivers:* rivers that flow across Iraq to the Persian Gulf

*stayed:* held back

*Muhammad:* (Mohammed) founder of the religion of Islam

*devout:* very religious

The Western Wall or Wailing Wall is a holy site for Jews. This 52-foot section of wall is all that is left of a Jewish temple that was destroyed by the Romans in A.D. 70.

War between the Arabs and the Israelis broke out soon after Israel was made a state in 1948. After that war, the Arabs controlled East Jerusalem and the Jews controlled West Jerusalem. In 1967 after more fighting, known as the Six-Day War, the Israelis claimed the entire city as well as two Arab territories on the borders of Israel. Conflict and fighting between Arabs and Jews in Palestine is still a problem today.

Excerpts from Grace Halsell, *Journey to Jerusalem* (New York: Macmillan, 1981), pp. 18–23, 99, 101–4. Reprinted by permission of the author.

# Growing Up in Cairo

"What a celebration took place on the day the Nile finally reached flood level."

**Jehan Sadat**

For thousands of years the Nile River has been a source of water, food, and transportation for the people of Africa.

*Shamm el-Nessim:* spring celebration

*secular:* not sacred

*abundance:* wealth

*barrage:* dam

*Cairo:* capital of Egypt

*silt:* soil carried by rivers

*Uganda and Ethiopia:* African nations

*Nilometer:* device that measures the Nile's water level

*Moses:* leader of the ancient Jews

*bulrushes:* tall water plants

*cubit:* ancient measure of length

*feluccas:* small, narrow ships

**W**ays of living and farming remained unchanged in Egypt for hundreds of years. Egyptians depended on the Nile River for successful crops. Not only was its water used for irrigation, but the Nile's yearly flood brought rich soil to the land. This flood was so important to the people of Egypt that it was marked by an annual holiday—Wafa' el-Nil. Jehan Sadat describes her childhood memory of celebrating Wafa' el-Nil. ∽

If **Shamm el-Nessim** was my favorite **secular** holiday in the spring, Wafa' el-Nil, **Abundance** of the Nile, was my favorite of late summer. On this day in August the **barrage** just south of **Cairo** would be cut, and the Nile, swollen with water and rich **silt** from its origins in **Uganda and Ethiopia**, would begin the annual two-month-long fall flood.

The best part of Wafa' el-Nil was that the festivities happened right on Roda Island. For days before, the *munadi el-Nil*, the crier of the Nile, had marched around our neighborhood, calling out the height the river had reached on the eighth-century **Nilometer** at the southern foot of our island, built on the spot where the infant **Moses** is believed to have been found in the **bulrushes**. Every day the crier in our district would

proclaim the level of the Nile closer to the sixteenth **cubit** on the Nilometer, a rise of over twenty feet from its normal level.

What a celebration took place on the day the Nile finally reached flood level. We knew it was time when we saw that the crier was accompanied by small boys banging on little drums and bearing brightly colored flags. "The river has given abundance and completed its measure," the crier would call out, to which the boys would reply, "God has given abundance!" They continued their call in front of each house until they were given a small present of money. And the festival began.

**Feluccas**, their riggings outlined in lights and dressed with colorful streamers and pennants, crowded into the Nile just off the shores of

70

Roda. Lights were strung on the shore as well. Some boats had musicians aboard, and from the shore we could hear the sounds of different songs echoing across the river. . . .

Tied to the pier at the foot of our island was a brightly painted boat bearing a large decorated statue of a girl known as the Bride of the Nile. When the flood started, the "bride" was thrown into the Nile at sunset to join her "bridegroom," thus ensuring a good harvest year. On the shore we all clapped and cheered and gave **tongue in the *zaghreet*** while fireworks were shot into the air. I loved the romance of their watery union, but was thankful that the "bride" was a statue now and not the young virgin that legend held Egyptians used to sacrifice annually years before.

When the completion of the **High Dam in Aswan** would eliminate the annual flood in 1964, I would be very sad that we stopped celebrating the Wafa' el-Nil. Its colorful traditions had already been eroded, the crier of the Nile having been replaced by flood-level updates on Cairo radio. But some of the legend of Wafa' el-Nil, at least, continues. **Lotuses**, the beautiful flowers that bloom in the . . . river, are still called "Brides of the Nile."

*tongue in the zaghreet:* high whistling sounds

*High Dam in Aswan:* dam across the Nile River at Aswan

*lotuses:* water lilies

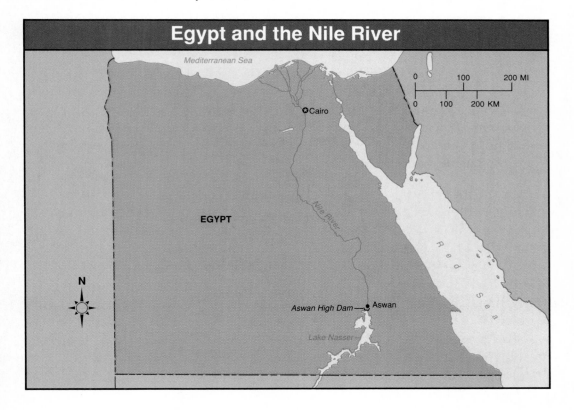

Egypt and the Nile River

The Aswan High Dam across the Nile was completed in 1970. It created a lake 300 miles long. Farmers irrigate their crops year round with water from the lake. And the dam provides hydroelectric power. But the dam did away with the yearly flood. Without the rich Nile silt, farmers downstream must use **fertilizers.** Also, without the yearly supply of new soil, the **delta** of the river is being **eroded**.

*fertilizers:* substances that enrich the soil

*delta:* low plain formed from sand, soil, and gravel deposited at the mouth of a river

*eroded:* worn or washed away

# The Saudi Arabian Way

" When dining on the floor, tuck your legs under you so the soles of your feet are hidden. "

**Alison R. Lanier**

**A**s the countries of North Africa and the Middle East have modernized, they have had more contact with the rest of the world. The huge oil business in Saudi Arabia brings business people from all over the world to that country. Knowing the customs of the country is helpful to people who do business in a foreign land. Alison Lanier, an author and teacher, explains Saudi Arabian ways for American business people. ∽

courteous: polite

*Gregorian Calendar:* the calendar introduced by Pope Gregory XIII in 1582 that is still used in many parts of the Western world

*the Prophet's Hegira:* (Hejira) Mohammed's journey to avoid capture

*Mecca:* holiest city of Islam, located in Saudi Arabia

*Medina:* holy city of Islam in Saudi Arabia

*Matters of Pace and Time*

The matter of pace is for many Westerners the *most* difficult adjustment to the Middle East. It has been said: "If you are in a hurry in the Middle East, don't bother." The Arab phrase is: "Haste comes from the Devil."

Patience is a master key for the area. If you wait patiently for an appointment—just settle down, stay there and wait—there will be no problem. When they get to you, they will be extremely **courteous**. They will expect you to be also, (no matter how tried your patience may be!). Visible annoyance will only be counter-productive; perhaps permanently so.

*Calendar*

The letters "A.H." mean Anno Hegirae, Year of the Hegira (or flight). They take the place of the Christian "A.D." in the **Gregorian Calendar**. Naturally, Muslims do not date their calendar by the birth of Christ, but by **the Prophet's Hegira** from **Mecca** to **Medina**—which took place in 622 (A.D.). One therefore adds 622 to their year to get the one familiar to us, i.e., our 1980 (A.D.) is their year 1358 (A.H.).

*Telling Time*

. . . The Arab day begins at sunset. This means that the night (of Monday let us say) precedes Monday rather than follows it, as is our custom. (Think of it as "the eve of Monday" as we speak of "Christmas Eve.")

*Official Holidays*

There are only two official holidays in the Kingdom for government and business:

(a) *Id Al-Fitr*—the end of **Ramadan**, the 9th month. This holiday runs three–five days and sometimes longer; most offices close two days before it starts.

(b) *Id Al-Adha*—The holiday connected with the Pilgrimage to Mecca and Medina—a feast of **penitence**, often about four days.

When making appointments, foreigners are advised to avoid both the above holidays by a few days before and after when planning any business. . . .

Be prepared also for the fact that devout Muslims pray five times a day. If they go to a nearby **Mosque**, rather than praying in their offices, each prayer session may be 20 to 30 minutes longer.

*Space: Getting and Keeping Attention*

Because of their heritage, Arabs have a noticeably different sense of space than those who come from crowded countries where space is carefully **allocated**. To Arabs space is public and there is lots of it.

Queuing up or standing in line [is] unheard of; whoever gets to a watering hole first—or to a taxi—wins. The same is true of conversations. Interrupting is not offensive if the interrupter has the priority and the right to do so. He will move in physically to talk at closer and closer range, partly to edge out anyone trying to horn in, but also partly because physical closeness is the way to be sure you are being heard.

Arabs carry on conversations from so close—about 10 inches—that they make most Europeans and North Americans uncomfortable (this is not a problem for South Americans who also like to stand close when they talk). The Arab conversational distance is about half of what is normally comfortable for most of the Western and Asian world. In addition, Arabs engage in much bodily contact. They like to tap a person, rest

*Ramadan:* month of fasting in the Muslim calendar

*penitence:* sadness or sorrow for having done something wrong

*Mosque:* Muslim holy temple

*allocated:* divided up

The Arabian city of Mecca was the birthplace of Mohammed. More than a million Muslims visit Mecca each year to worship at the Ka'aba, a small cube-shaped structure that holds a sacred stone.

Coffee is a favorite Arabian beverage. Here it is prepared in the traditional way in tall brass pots over an open fire.

a hand on a hand, an arm on an arm. This is taken as an assurance of attention or a means of emphasis, a way to make a point or express a feeling. But it is never done obviously, like slapping the back or prodding the ribs to emphasize a point or a joke.

The custom of the land is that men frequently hold hands, embrace warmly in public, or kiss one another on the cheek. An American reports having seen a **burly** soldier move his gun to the other hand so he could walk hand in hand down the street with a fellow soldier! This is the way of life there and does not have the **overtones** that it does in some cultures.

When talking, Saudis stand not only with their faces close together but with their bodies close as well, though not touching. Try not to draw back. This is their norm. Withdrawal to them will seem abnormal and a **rebuff**.

This different sense of space and the heritage of today's Arabs shows up also in the large size of their offices

and even more so in their philosophy of "out of sight, out of mind." Once you had disappeared into the shifting sands of the desert, no one thought of you again until you reappeared, if ever. The same is essentially true today. To get business done with an Arab, you—or your representative— need to maintain a constant physical presence. If you do not, little is likely to get done or someone else may take your place.

*Body Language*

Hands and gestures—as well as eyes—are used deliberately and carefully. Talking with one's hands, **gesticulating** widely, is considered to be impolite. Arabs keep the left hand for private functions and use the right for everything public. This includes eating, shaking hands, passing a document across the table (or money or a gift), etc. Foreigners should be extremely careful to do the same, *whether or not they are right-handed.* They should train themselves to keep both hands quiet as they talk, lest

*burly:*
big and strong

*overtones:*
suggested meanings

*rebuff:* rejection or rudeness

*gesticulating:*
making motions
with one's hands

their gestures be misunderstood, or, unwittingly, be in bad taste.

*Use of Names*

"Ibn" means "son of." Several generations may be added, as Hassan ibn Ulhman ibn Abdullah ibn Nasri. As a result it is not considered necessary to use a family name. (You will take a little time getting accustomed to the many Mohammads in your life!)

*Greeting Phrases*

It is important to learn the most common greeting phrases and replies even before you get to Saudi Arabia as you will need them at once. The rather lengthy sequence of greeting will be used when meeting a new business **colleague** as well as in routine greetings. It is standard. The very *least* you should do is say "good morning," (afternoon, evening) *and shake hands.* Individually greeting each person is required, even if it is necessary to use English. A general greeting for the whole room, such as "Hello everyone," will not do.

*Siesta Time*

One never visits a Saudi home between two–four P.M. This is **siesta** time and not to be invaded by anyone.

*Shoes and Feet*

A Muslim removes his shoes on entering a home and it is necessary for guests to follow this custom as well. When dining on the floor, tuck your legs under you so the soles of your feet are hidden. Watch how others are doing it. It is a serious insult to show the soles of your shoes or sandals to an Arab's face. If you are sitting opposite an Arab in a comfortable chair, be sure that your legs are not crossed in such a way that your shoe soles are pointed toward him. *Never* put your feet up on a stool, desk, train seat or any other raised surface.

**colleague:** associate; friend

**siesta:** rest, nap

Most Saudi men wear ankle-length gowns and a head covering. Many Saudi women wear veils to cover their faces.

Many American companies do business in Saudi Arabia. They offer special classes in Arabian culture. Oil is not the only reason foreign business people are attracted to Saudi Arabia. They also come to sell products such as soft drinks, cars, computers, and appliances. With the higher standard of living that oil has brought, Saudis are buying more of such products.

From Alison R. Lanier, *Saudi Arabia* (Yarmouth, Maine: Intercultural Press, 1981), pp. 31–33, 45–47, 77–79. Reprinted by permission.

# AFRICA SOUTH OF THE SAHARA

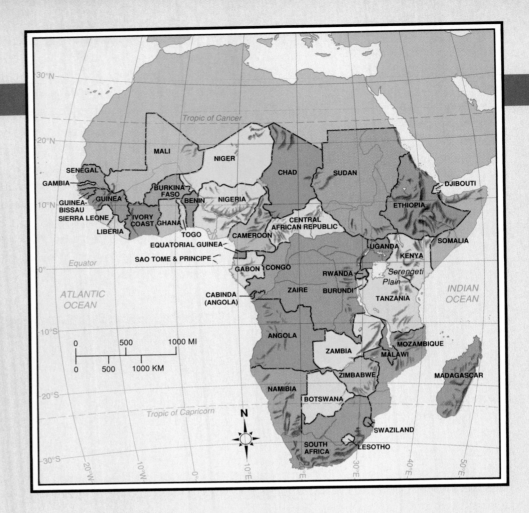

*rain forests:* dense woodlands that receive much rain

*savannas:* dry grassland areas with few trees

Imagine a desert bigger than the entire United States, a sea of sand and rock and gravel, where the sun's heat shimmers in waves and plays tricks on the eyes, where the clear night sky is peppered with stars. Such is the Sahara, the world's largest tropical desert. Its burning sands shift and spread over more than three million square miles of Africa. Once, very long ago, the land of the Sahara was green and fertile, a place where cities thrived and caravans of humpbacked camels swayed under their heavy loads. Today most of the land is not fit to live on.

The Sahara is a barrier that divides the vast continent of Africa into two main regions where people do live: sub-Saharan Africa and North Africa. Africa south of the Sahara is a complex region. Here there is almost no sameness—not in the land, not in the climate, not in the people. Kikuyu, Luyia, Kamba, Luo, Kalenjn, Masai, San, Khoikhoi, Fulani, Yoruba, Igbo, Hausa—these are only a few of the the many peoples who live here. There are probably more than 2,000 different groups in all living in more than 50 nations and speaking more than 800 different languages.

Scorching deserts, snow-dusted mountains, humid **rain forests**, and scrubby **savannas** are all part of the landscape of this massive continent that straddles the equator. Most of sub-Saharan Africa is a large, rolling plateau that ranges from hundreds to thousands of feet above sea level. But as the plateau stretches to the east, a series of deep, narrow valleys cuts across the face of the land from north to south. Known as the Great Rift Valley, these slashes in the earth's surface extend more than 3,000 miles—from the Red Sea, southwest through the eastern highlands of Ethiopia, and south across Kenya, Tanzania, and Malawi to Mozambique. In the Rift area are many deep gorges, churning rapids, and misty waterfalls.

Sub-Saharan Africa is an old land, rich in history and tradition. Here, four million years ago, the earliest known human beings made their home. Thousands of years ago, the rich trading kingdoms of Ghana, Mali, Songhai, Zimbabwe, and the Kush thrived here. Then, late in the 1800s, the Europeans came, lured by the wealth of the resources and the open land, and almost everything changed.

In Africa today, almost all the nations are independent. Africa is again a continent for Africans. Traditional ways survive in much of Africa. Villagers market their foods and wares from simple stalls. Farmers labor on the land, sowing the seeds, watching the skies, and waiting for the harvest. Herders tend their cattle, and the "talking drums" still beat a rhythm for daily life. But more than ever before, the people flock to the bright lights and traffic-jammed streets of cities like Nairobi, Lagos, and Harare, seeking a new kind of life.

This Nigerian potter uses clay to make sun-dried pots to sell in a village market. About three-fourths of the people in sub-Saharan Africa live in rural villages.

In this unit three people who grew up in Africa present some of the beauty and tradition of this diverse continent.

- In an interview, writer Chinua Achebe talks about growing up in **Nigeria.**
- Adventurer Beryl Markham describes the beauty and loneliness of the **Serengeti Plains**.
- Molapatene Collins Ramusi remembers his traditional wedding in **South Africa.**

# Nigerian Traditions

" . . . when you paid their debt then you became their king. "

**Chinua Achebe**

Nigeria has more people than any country in Africa. It is a country of contrasts with modern cities and country villages.

**M**any African nations were once European colonies. European rulers often discouraged the native African way of life. Many Africans are now trying to bring back native African traditions. One such person is Chinua Achebe, a respected Nigerian writer. In this interview he tells about his education and some of the customs of his people, the Igbo. The "participants" are people in the audience who asked him questions. ∽

PARTICIPANT:    I notice that you have written a story for children. I wonder if you would comment on the major writer's role or responsibility with respect to children in literature, since it does not happen too often?

ACHEBE:    Yes, I have written two books for children. The first one was prompted by Christopher Okigbo, the poet. . . . He came to me and said, "You must write a children's book because this is very important," and I'd never done it before. **I have a kind of missionary thing** about writing in addition to its pleasures, so I agreed with him that there was a need for this. I had seen it myself. I had seen it in my daughter who was growing up and for whom I was beginning to buy children's books. I never read those books myself when I was growing so I didn't know what

was in them. But I soon realized that my daughter was getting all kinds of wrong notions. This was in Nigeria, not in Europe or America. So one day I decided to look into these books, and, to give you a very quick rundown of the kind of story I saw, it is a story of a kite. There is a little boy, a white boy in Europe; you know, it's a glossy book, a lot of illustrations. You see the idea of Europe, town, big city, and this boy is flying a kite; and then the kite goes right up and gets caught in the tail of an **aeroplane** that is passing. And this aeroplane carries it and on and on and on, and somewhere far away this kite **dislodges** itself and begins to fall, and it falls into a coconut tree. And then you see the huts, the round huts, and a lot of **luscious** background; and then you see a little black boy, naked, climbing the coconut tree, and then

*I . . . thing:* I have a strong sense of purpose

*aeroplane:* airplane

*dislodges:* loosens; frees

*luscious:* beautiful, highly pleasing

halfway up he sees this kite, and so he is frightened, and he jumps down and calls his father who comes out with a spear and looks up and sees this kite; and he's scared and there's a big **to do** in the village. They send for the **witch doctor**, naturally. So the witch doctor comes with his group and a lot of drumming, and they dance around the tree seven times, and then the witch doctor's attendant climbs up and brings down this strange being with great **reverence**, and there is a big procession, and they take it to the village **shrine** where it is worshiped to this day. This is a very dangerous story. I don't think anyone has the right to tell children that kind of story about other people. Even if they had the right, I would not want my children to be brought up with that kind of story. This is the kind of feeling that set me going, and I found also it was interesting writing for children. It's very exciting. . . .

PARTICIPANT:   I'd like to ask you, in the educational system in your country, how much did you actually learn in terms of history as to the situation of blacks in America: how we came to be here, the type of treatment we received, and just the whole picture of slavery? I'd like to know how it was treated as a part of your education in your country.

ACHEBE:   Well when I was growing up, the educational system was very odd, to put it mildly. We did not study anything that had to do with us. The whole purpose of

*to do:* uproar; excitement

*witch doctor:* tribal spiritual leader

*reverence:* deep respect

*shrine:* altar; holy place

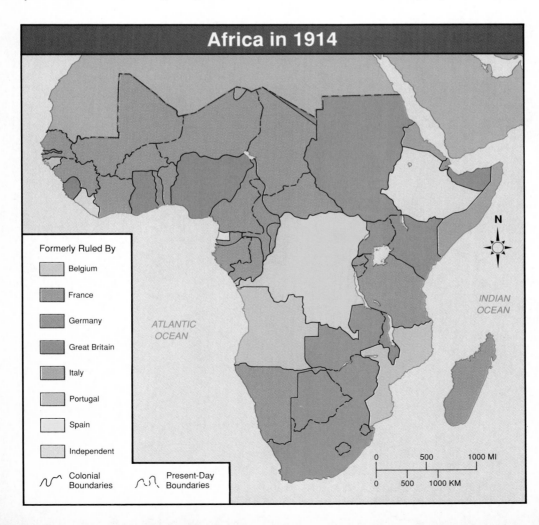

Africa in 1914

Formerly Ruled By

- Belgium
- France
- Germany
- Great Britain
- Italy
- Portugal
- Spain
- Independent

Colonial Boundaries

Present-Day Boundaries

ATLANTIC OCEAN

INDIAN OCEAN

N

0     500     1000 MI

0     500   1000 KM

primers: beginning
readers; elementary
textbooks

Gauls: warlike
people who
inhabited and
settled early France;
Europeans

Booker T.
Washington:
famous black
American leader
and educator. He
lived from 1856
to 1915.

constitutes:
forms; makes up

wives: In Igbo
culture men may
have more than
one wife.

destitute: very poor;
without money

in a material sense:
in terms of wealth
or possessions

titles: terms of
respect that tell a
person's status or
position

education seemed to be to tell you about other people so that the geography we did was the geography of England, the history we did was the history of England, and the constitution, well, even up to this day students take exams called "British Constitution." Then the French side was even worse. They had **primers** that began "Our ancestors the **Gauls**. . . ." So in that kind of setting there was no room for talking about slavery and that kind of thing. The first American book I read was in high school, and it was a sad book. It was *Up from Slavery* by **Booker T. Washington**, and this was a sad book, and that was all. Today I think it is different. Fortunately I think the educational system is much more rational, much more related to ourselves. Perhaps not as much as it ought to be, but it is certainly better than twenty years ago. . . .

PARTICIPANT:    What **constitutes** the definition of a good life?

ACHEBE:    I never thought of that. The good life. Well, let us say you are talking about somebody and you say "he's a man." That means the good life in my culture. He is honest, you can rely on his word; if he tells you "stand," it means "stand"; it does not mean run away. He should also be able to take care of his **wives** and children. In other words he is not **destitute**, because we have a proverb which says that a man who is in rags speaks words that are in rags, ragged words. So you are also to be to a certain extent successful, **in a material sense**. So both spiritual and material.

You couldn't take the **titles** in my culture if you were a thief. You couldn't. There is no way you could become a titled man if you were

Young students write on chalkboards in this village classroom. In Nigeria the government provides free elementary schools and supports five universities.

known to be dishonest in that sense. Also you were not allowed by this society to become too powerful, either politically or even economically. And the way they insure that you did not become a millionaire—we have no concept of millionaires—the way they insured this was to say to you, "If you want to prove that you are wealthy, then you must take titles." And so you say, "Oh yes, this is a very good idea; I'll take titles." Now the title taking will insure that you spend all your money. And this money will then go back into the community. You would feed the village for a number of days. You would give out money to those who had taken the title before you—a kind of social insurance. And by the end of this title you are **exhausted.** This is just the first title.

Now if you are still ambitious after that, you want to take the second, the next one, then in another five years they will say, "Fine, but these are the things you will do; you will feed the village for one week, and you will bring five cows"—or whatever it is—"to those who have this particular title." So you do that and by the end of this ceremony you are again **at par** with your neighbors. So in this kind of way you make sure that nobody becomes too powerful.

In fact the Igbos have a story about how they used to have the fifth

Many Nigerians live along the Niger River, the third largest river in Africa. The fertile soil around the river is used for raising crops.

title, the title of king, once in their system and the reason this title went out of use was that you were required to pay the debt of every member of your community before you could become their king. Once you do all the other things, then, as the last stage in this ceremony, all the community would come one at a time and tell you how much they owe, and when you paid their debt then you became their king. This is a very **profound** political statement.

Achebe's people, the Igbos, are the third largest group of people in Nigeria. The Igbos value freedom and self-government. They also value the history of their culture. Achebe says, "It was part of your education to know the story of your people." **Oral tradition** has kept Igbo history alive. But, according to Achebe, this tradition is changing. Many Igbo stories are now being written down for future generations.

*exhausted:* Here Achebe means "out of money."

*at par:* on the same level; equal

*profound:* deep; carefully thought out

*oral tradition:* passing on historical information by speaking rather than by writing

From *In Person: Achebe, Awoonor, and Soyinka,* ed. Karen Morell (Seattle: African Studies Program, University of Washington, 1975), pp. 29–30, 34–35, 41–42. Reprinted by permission.

# Flying Over Africa

" The Serengetti lay beneath me like a bowl whose edges were the ends of the earth. "

**Beryl Markham**

Serengeti National Park is a large wildlife preserve in Tanzania. It was created in 1940 to protect the animals that live there.

*Serengeti Plains/*
*Serengetti Plains:*
grassland in north central Tanzania with much wildlife

*Lake Nyaraza:*
now Lake Eyasi

*Tanganyika:*
a territory south of Kenya. Tanganyika merged with Zanzibar to form Tanzania in 1964.

*Kenya Colony:* In 1935, Kenya was a British colony. It became independent in 1963.

*Masai People:*
native people of East Africa

*benison:* blessing

*eland:* kind of antelope

*wildebeest:*
large antelope

*Rothschilds:*
wealthy European family

When East Africa was under British colonial control, many British people made a home there. Others came to hunt the wild game found in great numbers. Beryl Markham was born in England but grew up in Africa. From 1931 to 1936 she delivered mail, passengers, and supplies in East Africa in her small plane. In this reading she is flying over the **Serengeti Plains** in search of her missing friend Woody. ∞

The **Serengetti Plains** spread from **Lake Nyaraza**, in **Tanganyika**, northward beyond the lower boundaries of **Kenya Colony**. They are the great sanctuary of the **Masai People** and they harbour more wild game than any similar territory in all of East Africa. In the season of drought they are as dry and tawny as the coats of the lion that prowl them, and during the rains they provide the **benison** of soft grass to all the animals in a child's picture book.

They are endless and they are empty, but they are as warm with life as the waters of a tropic sea. They are webbed with the paths of **eland** and **wildebeest** and Thompson's gazelle and their hollows and valleys are trampled by thousands of zebra. I have seen a herd of buffalo invade the pastures under the occasional thorn tree groves and, now and then,

the whimsically fashioned figure of a plodding rhino has moved along the horizon like a grey boulder come to life and adventure bound. There are no roads. There are no villages, no towns, no telegraph. There is nothing, as far as you can see, or walk, or ride, except grass and rocks and a few trees and the animals that live there.

Years ago one of the banking **Rothschilds** on a hunting trip . . . pitched his tents in the Serengetti Plains near a huge pile of these rocks where there was protection from the wind and where there was water. Since then countless hunting parties on safari have stopped there, and Rothschild's Camp is still a landmark and a kind of haven for hunters who, coming so far, have for a while at least locked the comforts of the other world behind them.

There is no landing field at Rothschild's Camp, but there is a patch of ground flat enough to receive a plane if the wind is right and the pilot careful.

I have landed there often and usually I have seen lion in the path of my glide to earth. Sometimes they have moved like strolling dogs, indifferent and unhurried, or, upon occasion, they have taken time to pause and sit on their haunches, in cosy groups—males, females and cubs staring at the **Avian** with about the same expression one finds in the gold-framed family portraits of the **Mauve Decade**.

I do not suggest that the lion of the Serengetti have become so **blasé** about the modern explorer's motion-picture camera that their posing has already become a kind of Hollywoodian habit. But many of them have so often been bribed with fresh-killed zebra or other delicacies that it is sometimes possible to advance with photographic equipment to within thirty or forty yards of them if the approach is made in an automobile.

To venture that close on foot, however, would mean the sudden shattering of any kindly belief that the similarity of the lion and the pussy cat goes much beyond their whiskers. . . .

On the way from **Nungwe** I flew toward Rothschild's Camp because the spot was on Woody's route on his flight from **Shinyaga** in Western Tanganyika to **Nairobi** and I knew that, whether alive or dead, he would not be found far off his course.

He was flying a German **Klemm monoplane** equipped with a ninety-five horsepower British Pobjoy motor. If this combination had any virtue in such vast and unpredictable country, it was that the extraordinary wingspan

*Avian:*
Markham's plane

*Mauve Decade:*
reference to the 1890s in the U.S., a time when business grew and some families became very wealthy

*blasé:* unconcerned; bored

*Nungwe:* small outpost in the Kenyan wilderness

*Shinyaga:* (Shinyanga) city in Tanganyika (now Tanzania)

*Nairobi:* capital of Kenya

*Klemm monoplane:* kind of plane with only one pair of wings

The tall, dry grasses of the Serengeti are home to thousands of lions. Visitors can carry cameras but not guns when they travel through Serengeti National Park.

Masai women wear draped robes and layers of bright beaded necklaces. Many of the Masai people of Kenya are nomads.

of the plane allowed for long gliding range and slow landing speed.

Swiftness, distance, and the ability to withstand rough weather were, none of them, merits of the Klemm. Neither the plane nor the engine it carried was designed for more than casual flying over well-inhabited, carefully charted country, and its use by East African Airways for both transport and messenger service seemed to us in Kenya, who flew for a living, to indicate a some-what reckless persistence in the pioneer tradition.

The available aviation maps of Africa in use at that time all bore the **cartographer**'s scale mark, "1/2,000,000"—one over two million. An inch on the map was about thirty-two miles in the air, as compared to the flying maps of Europe on which one inch represented no more than four air miles.

Moreover, it seemed that the printers of the African maps had a slightly **malicious** habit of including,

in large letters, the names of towns, junctions, and villages which, while most of them did exist in fact, as a group of thatched huts may exist or a water hole, they were usually so **inconsequential** as completely to escape discovery from the cockpit.

Beyond this, it was even more **disconcerting** to examine your charts before a proposed flight only to find that in many cases the bulk of the terrain over which you had to fly was bluntly marked: "UNSURVEYED."

It was as if the mapmakers had said, "We are aware that between this spot and that one, there are several hundred thousands of acres, but until *you* make a forced landing there, we won't know whether it is mud, desert, or jungle—and the chances are we won't know then!"

All this, together with the fact that there was no radio, nor any system designed to check planes in and out of their points of contact, made it essential for a pilot either to develop his **intuitive sense** to the highest degree or to adopt a **fatalistic** philosophy toward life. Most of the airmen I knew in Africa at that time managed to do both.

Flying up from Nungwe on my hunt for Woody, I had clear weather and unlimited visibility. I stayed at an altitude of about five thousand feet. . . .

From the open cockpit I could see straight ahead, or peer backward and down, past the silver wings. The Serengetti lay beneath me like a bowl whose edges were the ends of the earth. It was a bowl full of hot vapours that rose upward in visible waves and exerted physical pressure against the Avian, lifting her, as heat from a smouldering fire lifts a flake of ash.

Time after time a rock, or a shadow, aided by my imagination, assumed the shape of a crumpled plane or a mass of twisted metal, and

I would **bank** and swing lower and lower over the suspected object until its outlines were sharp and clear—and disappointing again. Every foreign speck in the landscape became a Klemm monoplane come to grief, and every wind-inspired movement of a branch or a clump of bush was, for an instant, the excited signalling of a stranded man.

About noon I reached Rothschild's Camp and circled over it. But there was no activity, no life—not even the compact, slow-moving silhouette of a lion. There was nothing but the distinguishing formation of high, grey rocks piled against each other, jutting from the earth like the weather-worn ruins of a desert cathedral.

*bank:* tilt the plane so one wing is lower than the other

Visitors to the Serengeti National Park can see hundreds of different animals in the wild, including giraffes, wildebeests, and zebras.

Happily, Beryl Markham found Woody alive. They might be surprised to see the Serengeti today. Now 5,600 square miles of the area Markham flew over have been set off as a national park and wildlife area. Zebras, gazelles, and giraffes are some of the animals that live there. Because of too much hunting, many animals of the Serengeti were in danger of **extinction**. Although the animals are protected now, poaching, or illegal hunting, is a problem.

*extinction:* dying out altogether

Excerpted from *West With the Night*, copyright © 1942, 1983 by Beryl Markham, pp. 33–36. Published by North Point Press and reprinted by permission.

# A South African Wedding

" The crowd sang and danced to the traditional wedding songs. . . . "

**Molapatene Collins Ramusi**

About 2 million people live in the all-black city of Soweto. The city was built on barren land with few resources.

Families are very important in African cultures. The family unit includes all relatives. In some cultures, such as the Batlokwas in South Africa, families are joined into a **clan**. For these cultures, marriage is a way to increase family. Family members often help plan marriages. They also play an important role at weddings. In this reading a Batlokwa man tells how he courted and married a young woman he calls his "jewel." She belongs to another clan in a distant village. ∽

I asked my family to begin the traditional African marriage negotiations, which require *bohadi* (**dowry**) to be paid by the boy's family to the girl's family as a gift in consideration of the valuable addition of a wife to our family and the Babirwa clan—my clan. According to tradition, there could be no valid marriage between **Thabo** and me without payment of bohadi, but because Thabo's family were Christians, I sent my **emissaries** with no money or valuables, thinking they would not be expected.

My "**guardian angel**"; my cousin Motlatso Isaiah Maphala; and Robert Miyen, a friend and fellow **social worker**, traveled 600 miles to open marriage negotiations by asking for "a **calabash** of water," as my people say whenever they come to ask for a lady's hand in

marriage—the calabash from which we eat and drink.

Thabo's father, Sekgweng Morare, replied, "I have no mouth; I cannot speak. I have no eyes; I cannot see you. I have no ears; I do not hear"—he, in fact, required the traditional fee for "opening the mouths" of the girl's people. So my emissaries withdrew to **confer** among themselves. In recognition of the clan's relation to tradition, they delivered **5 pounds** cash and again asked for the calabash of water.

Thabo's father pretended to have no daughters and insisted that perhaps the girl they wanted lived next door. He encouraged the family to pretend that they did not want Thabo to be married. So the representatives of the two families talked back and forth until the Morare family

**conceded** and settled for the sum of 100 pounds as bohadi. . . .

Preparations for the wedding feast began in Thabo's village. The voices of the Batlokwa and Morare praise singers mingled in the yard on our wedding day, December 12, 1953. Thabo was a special bride. . . . A red carpet was laid for her on the path to the church. My mother stood **ululating** at the church door, chanting the praises of our clan, the Babirwa. My father's sister took over to praise my name. Then, at 11:00 A.M., Thabo and I were married. . . .

Aunt Malekanyane took over and praised my name. Then Sono's mother shouted, "We have taken her! We have taken her!" She announced to all present that Thabo was now married to our family, while Cousin Maphala and my guardian angel were jumping and kicking the dust in the manner of my people, who jump and dance in front of the bridal couple to show happiness at a wedding. The crowd sang and danced to the traditional wedding songs as we came out of the church.

I pounded the earth, kicked the dust, and danced. Thabo treaded softly amid the ululating voices of women from our two clans, the Elephant and Babirwa clans. I was happy. Thabo was happy.

*conceded:* yielded; gave up

*ululating:* wailing in a high voice

Soweto residents gathered to hear Nelson Mandela speak after his release from prison in 1990. Ramusi worked closely with Mandela, a leader in the struggle against apartheid in South Africa.

As a lawyer, Ramusi has spent his life fighting **apartheid** in South Africa. He spent eight years in the United States when he was forced to leave his own country. When he returned, he began to help his people fight the policy of race separation. He used legal and political means rather than violence. Violent opposition to white control has cost many lives. Ramusi himself lost a son in a violent protest against apartheid.

*apartheid:* policy of race separation

From *Soweto, My Love: A Testimony to Black Life in South Africa* by Molapatene Collins Ramusi and Ruth S. Turner, pp. 119–21. Copyright © 1989 by Molapatene Collins Ramusi. Reprinted by permission of Henry Holt and Company, Inc.

# SOUTH ASIA

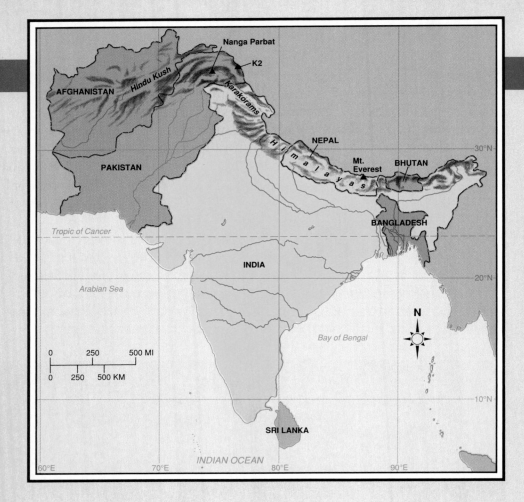

In the suffocating heat a peacock screams. Perhaps its call is an announcement. The land is dry and cracked. But today there is a new smell of dampness. The breezes start to blow, gently at first, then with a fury that swells and shoves the billowing clouds. Thunder claps and then booms. Lightning flashes and zigzags across the darkening skies. Finally it happens. Big drops of water splash down one by one. The drops pick up speed and a pelting sheet covers everything in sight. The people celebrate the rains with joy and relief.

This is the start of the rainy season in South Asia, brought by the seasonal winds called monsoons. Eighty percent of the rain falls in this season from mid-June to September. If the monsoon rains do not come to a region, crops fail and rivers shrink. In the **subcontinent** of South Asia, water, sacred and revered, is the key to life.

The subcontinent is separated from the rest of Asia by the knife-edged mountains of the Himalayas. The Himalayas are not one mountain range but several ranges that run parallel. Here cloud-capped mountains look down on unspoiled valleys and rushing rivers. The awesome Mount Everest, "Goddess of the Snows," challenges the world's toughest mountain climbers. The narrow, steep-walled Khyber Pass cuts through the mighty mountains. Connecting north Pakistan with Afghanistan, the pass was the only way migrating peoples

*subcontinent:* large landmass smaller than a continent

from Europe and northern invaders, in the long-ago past, could reach fertile India.

At the foot of the Himalayas is a flat, almost treeless crescent of rich land that reaches from Pakistan to Bangladesh. It is known as the Gangetic Plain. Through this plain run the three great rivers of South Asia—the Indus, the Brahmaputra, and the Ganges. Each of these rivers is fed by mountain snowfields and waters large areas of cropland with flooding. Cities with millions of people, such as Karachi, Calcutta, and Delhi, are found on the banks of these rivers.

South of the plain, on the triangle-shaped peninsula, the land is more varied. Old and weathered hills, low mountains, forest, and farmland make up the terrain. Underneath are rich mineral deposits that are just beginning to be mined. Because India makes up most of the land area and population of the subcontinent, this geographic feature is often called the Indian subcontinent.

The people of South Asia practice many religions. Hindus, Muslims, Buddhists, Christians, Sikhs, Jains, and Parsees all live here. Each group has its own way of life. Most people live in the country in villages where tradition is a strong force, where bulls still pull wooden plows and precious rainwater is collected and held in storage tanks until it is needed to water the fields. The rural life is hard. As the cities grow, they draw the young people from their homes to find excitement and the chance of a better life.

Most people who live in South Asia are farmers or craftspeople. This woman spins fibers into thread, which will be used for making cloth.

In this unit two people describe their observations about two very different aspects of South Asia.

■ In an interview, General Qamar Ali Mirza proudly describes the great mountain ranges near his home in **Pakistan**.

☐ Reflecting on a trip down the Ganges, British author Eric Newby explains why the river is so highly regarded by the people of **India** and **Bangladesh**.

# High in the Himalayas

" . . . climbers from all over the world thrill to the challenge of our mountains."

**Qamar Ali Mirza**

Few roads have been built to carry travelers through the jagged, snow-capped peaks of Pakistan.

*Kashmir:* region about the size of Utah in north India and northeast Pakistan

*porters:* local people who carry equipment and serve as guides

*Gilgit:* town on the Gilgit River in the Kashmir region of Pakistan

*base camp:* place partway up the mountain where supplies are kept

*summit:* highest point on a mountain

*K2:* second-highest mountain in the world

*Everest:* highest mountain in the world (29,028 feet)

*surveyed:* measured with scientific instruments

Every year mountain climbers from around the world come to **Kashmir** in South Asia. They come to climb some of the world's tallest mountains. But even expert climbers do not make the dangerous journey up the mountains without a guide. Retired General Qamar Ali Mirza was president of the Alpine Club of Pakistan, a club for mountain climbers. Here he provides a look at mountain climbing in Pakistan.

Some of the world's highest mountains are in Pakistan and people join our club to learn about mountaineering. Our mountain **porters** have been accompanying expeditions since the beginning of this century—mountaineering comes naturally to them. But now the sport is catching on with young Pakistanis, and our members often climb with foreign expeditions.

We run a training course near **Gilgit**, for high altitude porters. At present there are two types of porters: those who work up to the **base camp** and those who climb as professional guides all the way to the **summit**. They come from the villages of Baltistan and Hunza, in the Karakorams.

We have three great mountain ranges—the Karakorams, Himalayas and Hindu Kush. They lie alongside each other and it's hard to tell where one range begins and another ends. Five of the world's highest peaks are in Pakistan. Our biggest mountains are **K2**, 8,611 meters (28,253 feet) high, and Nanga Parbat, 8,125 meters (26,660 feet). K2 was first climbed by an Italian team in 1954—mountaineers say the mountain is a much greater challenge than **Everest**. Nanga Parbat is known as the Killer Mountain because it has claimed many lives, but it is regarded by many as the most beautiful and dramatic mountain in the world.

We have hundreds of mountains as high as 6,000 meters (20,000 feet). Many of the higher peaks have never been **surveyed**; their exact height is not known and they don't even have a name.

Baltoro Glacier, at the foot of K2, runs for more than 89 kilometers (55 miles). It looks like a smooth, glistening river of ice, and it has been slipping down the mountains for thousands of years.

Most of Pakistan's highest mountains are in the restricted area, near the disputed Kashmir border with India as well as China and Tibet, and climbers must have government permission to enter the area. They can climb any mountain up to 6,000 meters (20,000 feet) on their own if they wish, but for higher peaks the government insists on a party of at least four people, including a doctor and a government **liaison officer.**

In winter the snow comes down almost to 1,000 meters (3,289 feet); everything freezes and climbing is impossible. The climbing season is from mid-April to mid-October. The big peaks have ice all the year round and temperatures above 6,000 meters (20,000 feet) are many degrees below freezing. At these heights there is always a risk of **frostbite**, even on sunny days. Sometimes expeditions have to retreat because of bad weather. Fierce blizzards blow and it's easy to get lost and freeze to death, or fall off a cliff or down a **crevasse**.

But climbers from all over the world thrill to the challenge of our mountains. They all come with one common aim—to climb.

*liaison officer:* official who aids in communication between climbers and the government

*frostbite:* damage to a body part, such as the fingers or toes, caused by cold temperatures

*crevasse:* deep crack

Pakistani porters who live in the mountains are skilled rock climbers. They carry heavy loads through fast-moving mountain rivers and up steep mountain cliffs.

The Himalayas and other mountains in South Asia attract many visitors each year. These visitors bring needed money into the countries they visit. But tourism also brings problems. Some people who hike in the mountains leave trash. They also burn wood from the forests for fuel. This wood is an important resource for the mountain people. Many of the most popular hiking and climbing areas have been hurt by overuse.

Reproduced from *We Live in Pakistan*, pp. 16–17, by Mohamed Amin with the kind permission of Wayland (Publishers) Limited, 61 Western Road, Hove, BN3 1JD, England.

# The Ganges

" She is The Pure, The Eternal, The Light Amid the Darkness. . . . "

**Eric Newby**

The steps leading down to the Ganges River are called ghats. Hindus and Buddhists gather on the ghats to worship.

*monsoon:* periodic wind that usually brings heavy rainfall

*venerated:* honored

*pilgrimage:* religious journey

*meritorious:* deserving of praise

*cremated:* burned to ashes after death

*ejaculate:* speak in a burst

*100 leagues:* about 300 miles

*atone:* make up for

*three previous lives:* Hindus believe that each person has a series of lives.

*enumerate:* list

*metrically:* in a rhythmic word pattern, as in poetry

*She:* way of referring to the river as if it were alive

The Ganges River begins its journey of about 1,500 miles in the Himalayas. Flowing southeast, the Ganges snakes its way through India and Bangladesh. It is fed by melting snows and **monsoon** rains. In Bangladesh the Ganges joins with the Brahmaputra River. Then it flows into the Bay of Bengal. To the Hindus the waters of the Ganges are sacred. In this travel narrative, British author Eric Newby describes what he saw on a trip down the Ganges.

In most standard works of reference the Ganges does not even rate an entry in the tables which list the great rivers of the world, for it is only 1,500 miles long from its source in the Himalayas to the Bay of Bengal. The Nile, the Amazon, the Mississippi/Missouri are all more than two and a half times as long as the Ganges. The Irtysh and the Yangtze are both twice as long. The Congo, the Yellow River, the Mackenzie, the Niger, the Danube, the Euphrates, the Brahmaputra and the Indus, to name only a few, are all longer. But, all the same, it is a great river.

It is great because, to millions of Hindus, it is the most sacred, most **venerated** river on earth. For them it is *Ganga Ma*—Mother Ganges. To bathe in it is to wash away guilt. To drink the water, having bathed in it, and to carry it away in bottles for those who have not had the good fortune to make the **pilgrimage** to it is **meritorious**. To be **cremated** on its banks, having died there, and to have one's ashes cast on its waters, is the wish of every Hindu. Even to **ejaculate** *"Ganga, Ganga"*, . . . **100 leagues** from the river may **atone** for the sins committed during **three previous lives**.

In almost any bazaar in India one can buy a little, oblong paperback book. . . . It contains two works, bound up together. They are the *Gangastottara-sata-namavali* and the *Ganga-sahasra-nama-stotra*. They **enumerate** the 108 and the 1,000 names of the Ganges, all printed **metrically** and in columns so that they can be chanted. . . . **She** is The Pure, The Eternal, The Light Amid the Darkness, The Cow Which Gives

Much Milk, The Liberator, The Destroyer Of Poverty And Sorrow, The Creator of Happiness, to give only a few of her names.

The Ganges was not always so highly regarded. When the **Aryan invaders** first entered India they were more impressed by the Indus. It was only later that they gave *Ganga* the highest position, as *Sursari*, River Of The Gods—perhaps because they had found out what European scientists discovered later: that its water has remarkable **properties**. Bottled, it will keep for at least a year. At its **confluence** with the **River Jumna** which, particularly at the time of the great fair which takes place there every January, contains dangerous numbers of *coli*, the Ganges itself is said to be free of them. At **Banaras** thousands drink the water every day at bathing places which are close to the outfalls of **appalling** open drains. They appear to survive. The presence of large numbers of **decomposing** corpses seems to have no **adverse** effect on it. . . . Taken on board sailing ships in the **Hooghly** at **Calcutta** it is said to have outlasted all other waters. . . .

The Ganges first sees the light of day when it emerges from an ice cave above **Gangotri**, 13,800 feet up in the **Garhwal** Himalayas. Hindus believe that it was from this cave that *Ganga*, the daughter of King Himavat and the nymph, Mena, was persuaded to come down to earth by Bhagiratha, a descendant of King Sagar, in order to **redeem** from hell the souls of the sixty thousand sons of the king who had been reduced to ashes by a holy man whom they had **slighted**. . . .

For much of its course the Ganges is not a **navigable** river in the real sense of the word, although, in spite of the fact that millions of cubic feet of water are drawn off from it, its strength is constantly renewed by the rivers that flow into it. It is in the 600-mile stretch between **Allahabad**

| River Lengths | | |
|---|---|---|
| RIVERS LONGER THAN THE GANGES | | |
| Name | Location | Length (miles) |
| Nile | Africa | 4,132 |
| Amazon | South America | 4,000 |
| Yangtze | China | 3,915 |
| Mississippi/Missouri | United States | 3,741 |
| Yellow | China | 3,395 |
| Irtysh/Ob | Soviet Union | 3,361 |
| Congo | Africa | 2,900 |
| Mackenzie | Canada | 2,635 |
| Niger | Africa | 2,600 |
| Brahmaputra | Asia | 1,800 |
| Indus | Asia | 1,800 |
| Danube | Europe | 1,770 |
| Euphrates | Asia | 1,740 |

*Aryan invaders:* group of northern tribes that entered India about 1500 B.C.

*properties:* qualities

*confluence:* point of joining together

*River Jumna:* large river that flows into the Ganges

*coli:* bacteria that are sometimes harmful to people

*Banaras:* (or Benares) another name for Varanasi, an ancient holy city on the Ganges

*appalling:* shocking

*decomposing:* rotting

*adverse:* bad

*Hooghly:* important branch of the Ganges near its mouth at the Bay of Bengal

*Calcutta:* largest city in India

*Gangotri:* mountain temple in northern India

*Garhwal:* district of India that includes some of the Himalayas' highest mountains

*redeem:* release

*slighted:* insulted

*navigable:* deep enough to be used by boats

*Allahabad:* city where the Jumna flows into the Ganges

*Rajmahal:* region of hills south of the Ganges near the city of Patna

*silt:* particles of soil or sand

*Victorian:* period of history when Victoria was queen of Great Britain (1837-1901)

*Ghazipur:* town on the Ganges

*replicas:* copies

*alluvial:* river-carried

*delta:* triangle-shaped area at the mouth of a river, where it meets the sea

*Gangetic Plain:* broad area of fairly flat land on either side of the Ganges

*Kasimbazar:* town in the Delta region

*Bengal:* region of India that includes the Ganges Delta

*Warren Hastings:* British official in India in the early 1800s

*water hyacinth:* flowering water plant

*once-illustrious:* outstanding in the past

*Kanauj:* town in northern India near the Ganges

and **Rajmahal** that it really gathers strength. At Rajmahal, in full flood, it goes down at 1,000,800 cubic feet a second which is greater than the maximum discharge of the Mississippi. . . . Fortunately it brings down with it vast quantities of **silt** which it deposits free of charge for a season before sweeping it further downstream. A **Victorian** engineer, Sir Charles Lyell, estimated that 335,000,000 tons of silt were discharged each year at **Ghazipur** on the Middle Ganges. "Nearly the weight of sixty **replicas** of the Great Pyramid." . . . No one knows for certain the depth of the **alluvial** silt in the **Delta**. . . .

The Ganges is always trying to straighten itself out. It sets its current strongly against one bank, undercutting it and leaving sluggish water on the other shore on which new deposits are made, until it finally breaks

through and begins the whole process afresh. The **Gangetic Plain** is riddled with old, dead watercourses that the Ganges has forgotten about. At **Kasimbazar** in **Bengal**, where one of the first British trading stations was established in 1658, there is a flight of steps from which it is said that **Warren Hastings** used to come ashore. Only the river has gone, leaving a few pools choked with **water hyacinth**. The **once-illustrious** city of **Kanauj** on the Upper Ganges is now so far from the actual stream that, passing it in a boat in the dry season, one does not realise that it is there at all. . . . Four hundred miles out in the Bay of Bengal the sea is discoloured by the silt brought down by it. The Ganges justifies the one hundred and second name given it in the *Gangastottara-sata-namavali*— "Roaming About Rose-Apple-Tree Island," which is India.

In the holy city of Banaras (or Varanasi) the Ganges is lined with Hindu temples. Worshipers on the ghats shade themselves from the hot sun with large umbrellas.

## Indian Names for the Ganges

| Indian Name | Meaning |
| --- | --- |
| Visnu-padabja-sambhuta | Born from the lotus-like foot of **Vishnu** |
| Himacalendra-tanaya | Daughter of the Lord of Himalaya |
| Sughosa | **Melodious** (or: Noisy) |
| Sindhu-gamini | Flowing to the ocean |
| Bhagyavati | Happy, fortunate |
| Ksira-subhra | White as milk |
| Naga-putrika | Daughter of the mountain |
| Nitya-suddha | **Eternally** pure |
| Ramya | Delightful |
| Bindu-saras | River made of water-drops |
| Amrtakara-salila | Whose water is a mine of **nectar** |
| Lila-lamghita-parvata | Leaping over mountains in sport |
| Sankha-dundubhi-nisvana | Making a noise like a **conch-shell** and drum |
| Bhagya-janani | Creating happiness |
| Siddha | Perfect, holy |
| Sarac-candra-nibhanana | Resembling the autumn moon |
| Daridrya-hantri | Destroyer of poverty |
| Saranagata-dinarta-paritrana | Protector of the sick and suffering who come to you for **refuge** |
| Puratana | Ancient |
| Japa | Muttering, whispering |
| Jangama | Moving, alive |
| Jambu-dvipa-viharini | Roaming about (or delighting in) Rose-apple-tree Island (India) |

*Vishnu:* one of the most important Hindu gods

*melodious:* having a pleasing melody

*eternally:* forever

*nectar:* sweet-tasting drink

*conch-shell:* spiral shell of a small marine animal

*refuge:* shelter or protection

The Ganges River is not only a place for worshipping. It is a life-giving river that makes the Ganges Basin one of the richest farming areas in the world. Rice, wheat, barley, and sugar cane are grown there. The Indian government plans to build a canal to extend the Ganges into the southern half of India. The canal will irrigate large areas that do not now have enough water. And it will help solve drought problems during the dry season.

Excerpts from *Slowly Down the Ganges* by Eric Newby, pp. 15–22. Copyright © 1966, 1983 by Eric Newby. Reprinted by permission of Collins Publishers, London, England.

# UNIT 8

# SOUTHEAST AND EAST ASIA

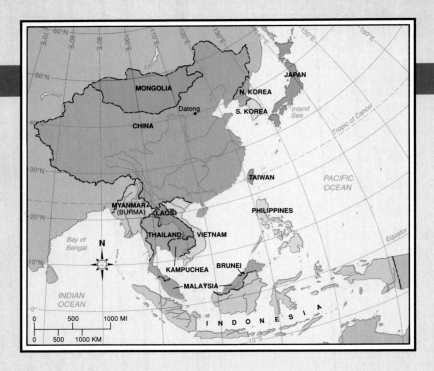

*Indochina:* geographers' term for the region that includes Burma, Thailand, Laos, Vietnam, Kampuchea, and West Malaysia

"Land Under Heaven," "Land of the Rising Sun," "Kingdom of a Million Elephants." These colorful names describe countries in Southeast and East Asia. "Land Under Heaven" is the name the early Chinese gave to their fertile land in the valley of the Hwang Ho River more than 4,000 years ago. "Land of the Rising Sun" describes Japan, said in the old myths to be favored by the sun goddess and ruled by her descendants. "Kingdom of a Million Elephants" refers to Laos, a country where elephants run wild and many are trained to carry heavy loads for people. The people who lived in these countries bestowed these names to show that they felt blessed with the resources of their beautiful lands.

The region of Southeast and East Asia is a combination of large land masses, peninsulas, and islands. The largest country in the region, China, has several different climates. The desert-covered northwest has cold winters and hot summers. The northeastern coast has a climate similar to the American Midwest. The moist, subtropical climate of the southern coast extends to all the countries of **Indochina**. In this climate area, most of the world's rice is grown. Farmers plant the rice in the standing water of wide paddies and on carefully terraced fields that look like giant curving stairsteps up the mountainside.

Rivers abound in the region. The Irrawaddy, the Mekong, and the Chao Phraya flow through the Indochina peninsula. Two of the mightiest and most historic rivers flow through China. The Hwang Ho, or the Yellow River, is also called the "River of Sorrows" because of its destructive floods. The Yangtze is the longest river in Asia and the third longest in the world. Small craft powered by sails or oars carry people and goods on this swift river.

Mountains have formed in nearly every country of Southeast and East Asia. Some are tall and jagged. Some have been worn down with

96

time. Some are bare and rocky. Others are forested with pines and birches and prickly junipers. Some, such as Mount Fuji in Japan, are perfect volcanic cones. Many volcanoes are active, such as Indonesia's Gunung Agung, which natives call the "navel of the world."

Southeast and East Asia is a region packed with people. There are a billion people in China alone. Muslims, Buddhists, Confucianists, Catholics, and Shintoists all live here. The ear cannot begin to pick out all the languages. There are two worlds here. There is the old world of custom and heritage, of straw and mud houses, of planting, weaving, and carrying water by hand, of revering ancestors and the natural world. There is the new world of technology—of the microchip, the motor scooter, and the neon sign, of international trade and modern universities and hospitals. But somehow these elements hold together. There is, as described in the national motto of Indonesia, "unity in diversity."

In Japan a large crowd gathers on the streets of Tokyo to celebrate May Day. An average of 850 people live on each square mile of land in Japan.

In this unit four writers depict life in different parts of Southeast and East Asia.

- Paul Theroux takes a ride on the train through northern **China** to the Datong Locomotive Works.
- Donald Keene describes the busy and breathtaking Inland Sea in **Japan.**
- An American writer, Norma Bixler, gives a picture of **Burma** (now Myanmar) through its three seasons.
- In a memoir, Le Ly Hayslip describes her childhood on a rice farm in central **Vietnam.**

# China
# by Train

"It was the Chinese who came up with the first design of the steam engine in about A.D. 600."

**Paul Theroux**

Mongolians raise camels, horses, and other livestock on the vast rolling prairies of Inner Mongolia in northeastern China.

*semi-arid:* somewhat dry

*province:* political unit of a country

*town:* Erlian, a town in Inner Mongolia

*shunted:* switched from one track to another

*hoisting:* lifting

*frugally:* not wastefully

*Great Wall:* wall built entirely by hand between the third century B.C. and A.D. 1600 to protect China's northern border from invaders. The main part of the wall is about 2,000 miles long.

*commune:* community in which the people share work and the ownership and use of property

**B**y size, China is the third largest country in the world. It is the largest country in population. Because of its immense size, China's geography changes greatly from region to region. In the northern, **semi-arid province** of Shanxi, the land is rich in coal and iron ore. Factories and mines are common sights. In 1976 Paul Theroux traveled through this province along one of China's many railroad lines. The train stopped in the city of Datong, home of a remarkable train factory.

It was a very hot day in May, and the whole **town** shimmered in the heat. . . . The train was **shunted** into the shed to have its wheels changed. But it was not just the wheels—the whole undercarriage was unbolted and replaced, Chinese-style, by **hoisting** the train, looping it with cables and pulling it apart until ninety tons of cast iron were swinging back and forth. . . .

I walked around for three and a half hours, waiting for the train to return with new wheels. . . .

We set off again, to cross the plains. It was a long hot afternoon, with only the merest glimpse of people or animals. I saw camels grazing, and herds of horses, and sparrow hawks. At the railway stations with Mongolian names— Qagan Teg and Gurban Obo—the

buildings were **frugally** built but freshly painted, with tiled roofs and flared eaves. . . . Towards dusk there were hills in the distance, the limit of the province of Inner Mongolia and the beginning of Shanxi.

That provincial border is marked by a section of the **Great Wall**. We clattered along the Wall for a while and then, in darkness, passed through it. The Wall is broken and sloping and piled up here—a muddy-looking heap of brown bricks and rubble. We had arrived at the big brown city of Datong. . . .

We were taken to the locomotive works, which was one of those Chinese factories that is so self-contained it is like a city. It was formerly a **commune**; it had schools and a hospital and stores, and a wall around it. It had a hotel, The Datong

Locomotive Works Hotel, and that was where we stayed. . . .

There were people working by the roadside—tinsmiths, carpenters, people drying beans and washing clothes and processing rags and sorting spinach. And repairing vehicles: it is the commonest sight on a Chinese road, people pumping tires, or fiddling with engines, or welding an axle; the bus jacked up and the mechanic's legs sticking out from under it.

The yellow smog in Datong was a combination of desert dust and fog and industrial smoke. It is a coal-burning city, and one of the largest open-pit mines in China is just outside the city limits. The fog was thick and **sulphurous** in the early morning, and it made the buildings look ghostly and ancient and the people **wraithlike**. But the buildings

The Great Wall of China was originally built to keep out barbarian invaders. The wall is almost 4,000 miles in length.

weren't old and the people were well fed and fairly friendly. . . .

The Chinese are the last people in the world still manufacturing **spittoons**, **chamber pots**, **treadle sewing machines**, bed warmers, "quill" pens (steel nibs, dunk-and-write), wooden yokes for oxen, iron plows, **sit-up-and-beg bicycles**, steam engines, and the **1948 Packard** car (they call it "The Red Flag").

They still make grandfather clocks—the chain-driven mechanical kind that go *tick-tock* and *bong!* Is this interesting? I think it is, because the Chinese invented the world's first mechanical clock in the late **Tang Dynasty**. [The Chinese forgot about it, like] many other Chinese inventions, . . . lost the idea, and the clock was reintroduced to China from Europe. The Chinese were the first to make cast iron, and soon after invented the iron plow. Chinese **metallurgists** were the first to make steel ("great iron"). The Chinese invented the crossbow in the fourth century B.C. and were still using it in 1895. They were the first to notice that all snowflakes have six sides. They invented the umbrella, the **seismograph**, **phosphorescent** paint, the spinning wheel, sliding **calipers**, **porcelain**, the magic lantern (or **zoetrope**) and the stink bomb. . . . They made the first kite, 2000 years before one was flown in Europe. They invented movable type and devised the first printed book . . . in the year 868. They had printing presses in the eleventh century, and there is clear evidence that **Gutenberg** got his technology from the Portuguese who in turn had learned it from the Chinese. They constructed the first suspension bridge and the first bridge with a segmented arch (this first one, built in 610 is still in use). They invented playing cards, fishing reels and whiskey.

*sulphurous:* (sulfurous) greenish-yellow

*wraithlike:* ghostlike

*spittoons:* containers into which people spit

*chamber pots:* small portable toilets

*treadle sewing machines:* sewing machines powered by a foot lever

*sit-up-and-beg bicycles:* bicycles with flat seats and turned-up handles

*1948 Packard:* an American luxury car

*Tang Dynasty:* period when the Tang family ruled China, A.D. 618–907

*metallurgists:* metal experts

*seismograph:* instrument that measures and records ground movement, such as earthquakes

*phosphorescent:* glowing

*calipers:* instruments that measure thickness and diameter

*porcelain:* hard ceramic material

*zoetrope:* toy with moving pictures

*Gutenberg:* (Johann) first European to print with movable type minaret: slender tower on top of a Muslim place of worship

Canton (Guangzhou): large city in southeast China

lacquer: shiny coating often painted on furniture

Turfan: northern Chinese city

impervious: incapable of being pierced

In the year 1192, a Chinese man jumped from a **minaret** in **Canton (Guangzhou)** using a parachute, but the Chinese had been experimenting with parachutes since the second century B.C. Gao Yang (reigned 550-559) tested "man-flying kites"—an early form of hang glider—by throwing condemned prisoners from a tall tower, clinging to bamboo contraptions; one flew for two miles before crash landing. The Chinese were the first sailors in the world to use rudders; Westerners relied on steering oars until they borrowed the rudder from the Chinese in about 1100. Every schoolboy knows that the Chinese invented paper money, fireworks and **lacquer.** They were also the first people in the world to use wallpaper (French missionaries brought the wallpaper idea to Europe from China in the sixteenth century). They went mad with paper. An excavation in **Turfan** yielded a paper hat, a paper belt and a paper shoe, from the fifth century A.D. . . . They also made curtains and military armor of paper—its pleats made it **impervious** to arrows. Paper was not manufactured until the twelfth century in Europe, about 1200 years after its invention in China. They made the first wheelbarrows, and some of the best Chinese wheelbarrow designs have yet to be used in the West. . . .

It was the Chinese who came up with the first design of the steam engine in about A.D. 600. And the Datong Locomotive Works is the last factory in the world that still manufactures steam locomotives. China makes big, black choo-choo trains, and not only that—no part of the factory is automated. Everything is handmade, hammered out of iron, from the huge boilers to the little

The Chinese were the first to develop a technique for making silk from the cocoons of silkworms.

The locomotive factory in Datong still produces steam-powered locomotives used to power China's trains.

brass whistles. China had always imported its steam locomotives—first from Britain, then from Germany, Japan and Russia. In the late 1950s, with Soviet help, the Chinese built this factory in Datong, and the first locomotive was produced there in 1959. There are now 9000 workers, turning out three or four engines a month, what is essentially a nineteenth-century vehicle, with a few refinements. Like the spittoons, the sewing machines, the washboards, the yokes and the plows, these steam engines are built to last. They are the primary means of power in Chinese railways at the moment, and although there is an official plan to phase them out by the year 2000, the Datong Locomotive Works will remain in business. All over the world, **sentimental** steam railway enthusiasts are using Chinese steam engines, and in some countries—like Thailand and Pakistan—most trains are hauled by Datong engines. There is nothing Chinese about them, though. They are the same gasping locomotives I saw shunting in Medford, Massachusetts, in 1948, when I stood by the tracks and wished I was on them.

*sentimental:* romantic; nostalgic

Beginning in the late 1940s, Chinese leaders decided to change China from a farming country to an industrial power. This decision led to the expansion of China's out-of-date railway system. The miles of railroad tracks in China grew from 13,500 in 1949 to about 33,000 today. The Chinese depend on the railways for traveling and for shipping raw materials, food, and industrial goods across their vast country.

Reprinted by permission of The Putnam Publishing Group from *Riding the Iron Rooster* by Paul Theroux, pp. 66–71. Copyright © 1988 by Cape Cod Scriveners Co.

# Japan's Inland Sea

" . . . for scenic beauty the Inland Sea is still a match for anywhere in the world I know."

**Donald Keene**

The Inland Sea of Japan is a major shipping channel bordered by three of Japan's four largest islands.

Japan is an island country off the east coast of the Asian continent. It is made up of four large islands and over 3,000 smaller ones. Mountains cover more than two-thirds of the islands. Most Japanese people live on the narrow coastal plains and lowlands. Japan's large southern islands nearly surround a magnificent body of water. This Inland Sea is 40 miles wide and 270 miles long. ∽

No region of Japan gives more immediate pleasure than the Inland Sea. From the deck of the ferry or speedboat, patterns of islands change **kaleidoscopically**, now linking together to form a single **serrated** island, now standing apart as if to allow fishing boats and tankers to pass. . . . Even if it is raining, the varied shapes of the islands, dimly visible through the mist, claim your entire attention.

The Inland Sea is usually calm, more like a lake than a sea, because it is all but encircled by the main islands—Honshu to the north, and Shikoku and Kyushu to the south and west. The view is so entrancing that it's easy to forget that this is not simply a magnificent tourist attraction, but a much-used waterway dotted with entirely businesslike ships of many sizes and nationalities. The scene changes constantly,

each turn on the way revealing another surprising cluster of islands and ships. . . .

According to Japanese mythology, the islands of the Inland Sea are the oldest part of the country. In historical times the area around the Inland Sea was the scene of all three great battles of the civil war of the 12th century between the **Heike and Genji clans**, a bitter struggle that involved the whole country and ended with the total destruction of the once-**omnipotent** Heike. More recently, it was on an Inland Sea city, Hiroshima, that the first atomic bomb was dropped. The extraordinary postwar growth of the Japanese economy can be **surmised** from the huge industrial complexes along the coast, notably the immense automobile works outside Hiroshima where Mazda cars are manufactured.

In the past, travelers from China

*kaleidoscopically:*
constantly forming new patterns or colors

*serrated:* regularly notched or toothed

*Heike and Genji clans:* two Japanese ruling families

*omnipotent:*
all-powerful

*surmised:* guessed

or elsewhere in Asia usually reached Japan by way of the Inland Sea. Their ships would pass through the Strait of Shimonoseki, where Honshu and Kyushu come close together, then make their way across the sea to Kobe or some other port. Nowadays travelers are much more likely to arrive by air in **Tokyo** or Osaka, and if they decide to visit the Inland Sea, they will start at the eastern, or Awaji, end. . . .

The islands of the Inland Sea do not contain cultural riches of the kind you find in **Kyoto** or **Nara**. Their inhabitants have always been few, and most **eked out** a bare living until the recent economic developments that brought to the islands the advantages (and disadvantages) of the cities. The waters of the Inland Sea are no longer pure, and some islands have been marred by ugly new buildings. But the whole is greater than the sum of its parts: almost every island is lovely, and for scenic beauty the Inland Sea is still a match for anywhere in the world I know.

*Tokyo:* Japan's capital city

*Kyoto:* major southern Japanese city; Japan's capital, 794–1868

*Nara:* southern Japanese city; Japan's capital, 710–784

*eked out:* earned with great effort

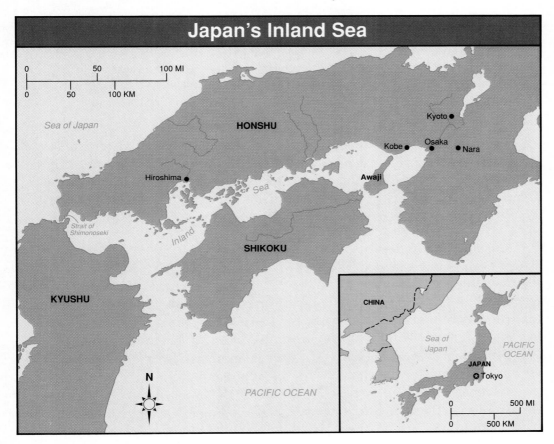

The area around the Inland Sea is a major center of Japanese industry. From these seaports, ships carry products such as iron, steel, chemicals, petroleum, and coal to the rest of the world. The Inland Sea is also a center for tourism. Tourists travel by ferry to big coastal cities and to some of the smaller islands. To protect it from industrial growth, the Japanese have set aside much of the Inland Sea as a national park.

# A Year in Burma

" In general there are three seasons in Burma, the cool, the rainy and the hot. . . . "

**Norma Bixler**

A Buddhist pagoda rises above the treetops near a field where two farmers prepare the land for planting.

*Burma:* name changed to Myanmar in 1989

*Himalayas:* mountain range in southern Asia

*Malaya:* formerly a country in southeast Asia; now part of Malaysia

*inexorably:* without stopping

The summer monsoons in Southeast Asia are very strong windstorms. They bring with them rains that can last for weeks. The people of **Burma** think of the monsoons as a gift of life. After a long, hot dry season, the rains flood the fields. Then people work quickly to plow their fields and plant rice. Norma Bixler, an American who lived in Burma, describes the seasons. ⬯

Burma isn't large—about the size of Texas—but it is long. Roughly diamond-shaped, its northern point reaches almost to the lashing tail of the **Himalayas**, though few people live there. A narrow throat of land stretches down toward **Malaya**, within ten degrees of the equator. . . .

In general there are three seasons in Burma, the cool, the rainy and the hot, and . . . in general these are the three seasons of Southeast Asia.

The monsoon rains end in October; by mid-November, when the earth has somewhat dried out and stopped steaming, the world is a beautiful place. The sky is an incredible blue in a high curve above the earth. These are the months of growth. The rice paddy is a delicate spring green, the grain not yet headed out, and there are miles and miles of it. Rivers, ponds and

irrigation ditches are full of life-giving water. . . .

By Christmas, the cool season has really come, a little too cool for the Burmese, a delightful time for Westerners. Thermometers drop to 68° at night, rise to no more than 90° at high noon. . . .

By March, occasional days are beginning to be hot before noon and you wait for the coolness to come back and then realize suddenly that it won't be back. . . .

After that the heat increases **inexorably**, all through April and the first half of May, . . . though there aren't yet any rains. The earth dries and cracks in the bare paddy fields. . . . Grass and ground-cover withers and dies; on every slope, the earth is bare and without defense against the rains that are coming. . . .

Then at last the monsoons are

here. The sky is gray, the wind blows, the rain runs like rivers. . . .

With the rains, the dust turns to mud in village compounds, along jungle paths, along the roads. Sometimes the rain turns the mud to soup and then, in the villages, as it rises, transforms the whole compound to a stagnant pond. . . .

And now it is time to work again. First, the plowing and the rice seeds in the seedbeds, then the back-breaking transplanting of the seedlings into the flooded beds, the careful adjustment of the water in the small fields. . . .

The whole cycle has begun again, the **mystical** union between the peasant and the rice. For rice has a meaning to these people which no food, not even corn or wheat, has to us. They eat it three times a day and they eat it, if they have it, in large quantities. Nationally, to a rice-exporting land like Burma, it is not only food but **foreign exchange**, money to buy **lorries** and machinery and mills for the economic takeoff they hope to reach, to buy for the people the everyday necessities which Burma can't yet supply for herself.

*mystical:* spiritual

*foreign exchange:* money used to buy goods from foreign countries

*lorries:* trucks

After harvesting their crops, farmers who live along Burma's rivers sell their produce at floating markets.

Rice is Burma's main food supply. It is also Burma's most important export. If the rice crop fails, the country suffers badly. Recently a number of farmers put in their own irrigation systems. These allow the farmers to plant crops, such as tomatoes and corn, even during the dry season. As irrigation becomes more widely used, Burma will no longer have to depend on just one crop.

From Norma Bixler, *Burmese Journey* (Yellow Springs, Ohio: Antioch Press, 1967), pp. 180–84. Reprinted by permission of Jon Bixler.

# A Rice Farm in Vietnam

" . . . because each grain was a symbol of life, we never wasted any of it."

**Le Ly Hayslip**

Farmers plant rice seedlings in fields flooded with water in the Mekong River delta in southern Vietnam.

The economy of Vietnam depends on agriculture, especially rice. Vietnam ranks sixth among the world's leading rice-growing countries. Its fertile land and hot climate are perfectly suited for rice farming. More than an export, rice is the main staple of the Vietnamese diet. Most Vietnamese eat rice at every meal. In her memoir, Le Ly Hayslip describes what it was like to grow up on a rice farm in Vietnam. ∽

*Ky La:* rice-farming village in central Vietnam

*taro:* plant with a starchy edible root

*fickle:* unpredictable

*mallets:* hammers with large heads

*conveyed:* carried

Although we grew many crops around **Ky La**—sweet potatoes, peanuts, cinnamon, and **taro**—the most important by far was rice. Yet for all its long history as the staff of life in our country, rice was a **fickle** provider. First, the spot of ground on which the rice was thrown had to be just right for the seed to sprout. Then, it had to be protected from birds and animals who needed food as much as we did. As a child, I spent many hours with the other kids in Ky La acting like human scarecrows—making noise and waving our arms—just to keep the raven-like *se-se* birds away from our future supper. . . .

When the seeds had grown into stalks, we would pull them up—*nho ma*—and replant them in the paddies—the place where the rice

matured and our crop eventually would be harvested.

After the hard crust had been turned and the clods broken up with **mallets** to the size of gravel, we had to wet it down with water **conveyed** from nearby ponds or rivers. Once the field had been flooded, it was left to soak for several days, after which our buffalo-powered plows could finish the job. In order to accept the seedling rice, however, the ground had to be *bua ruong*—even softer than the richest soil we used to grow vegetables. We knew the texture was right when a handful of watery mud would ooze through our fingers like soup.

Transplanting the rice stalks from their "nursery" to the field was primarily women's work. Although

| World's Leading Rice Growers | |
| --- | --- |
| COUNTRY | AMOUNT OF RICE PRODUCED IN 1987 (metric tons) |
| China | 177 million |
| India | 78 million |
| Indonesia | 39 million |
| Bangladesh | 22 million |
| Thailand | 18 million |
| Vietnam | 15 million |
| Myanmar (Burma) | 14 million |
| Japan | 13 million |

we labored as fast as we could, this chore involved bending over for hours in knee-deep, muddy water. No matter how practiced we were, the constant search for a foothold in the sucking mud made the **tedious** work exhausting. Still, there was no other way to transplant the seedlings properly; and that sensual contact between our hands and feet, the baby rice, and the wet, receptive earth, is one of the things that preserved and heightened our connection with the land. . . .

When the planting was done, the ground had to be watered every other day and, because each **parcel** had supported our village for centuries, fertilized as well. Unless a family was very wealthy, it could not buy chemicals for this purpose, so we had to shovel manure from the animal pens and carry it in baskets to the fields where we would cast it evenly onto the growing plants. When animals became scarce later in **the war,** we sometimes had to add human waste collected from the latrines outside the village. And of course, wet, fertile ground breeds weeds and pulling them was the special task of the women and children. . . . The standing water was also home for mosquitoes, **leeches**, snakes, and freshwater crabs and you were never too sure just what you would come up with in the next handful of weeds. It was backbreaking, unpleasant labor that ran fourteen hours a day for many days.

When the planting was over, we would sit back and turn our attention to the other tasks and rewards of village life: from making clothes and mending tools to finding **spouses** for **eligible** children and honoring our ancestors in a variety of rituals. . . .

Beginning in March, and again in August, we would bring the mature rice in from the fields and process it for use during the rest of the year. In March, when the ground was dry, we cut the rice very close to the soil—*cat lua*—to keep the plant alive. In August, when the ground was wet, we cut the plant halfway up—*cat gat*—which made the job much easier.

The separation of stalk and rice was done outside in a special smooth area beside our house. Because the rice was freshly cut, it had to dry in the sun for several days. At this stage, we called it *phoi lua*—not-yet rice. The actual separation was done by our water buffalo, which walked in lazy circles over a heap of cuttings until the rice fell easily from the stalks. We gathered the stalks, tied them in bundles, and used them to fix roofs or to kindle our fires. The good, light-colored rice, called *lua chet,* was seperated from the bad, dark-colored rice—*lua lep*—and taken

*tedious:* tiresome

*parcel:* small piece of land

*the war:* the Vietnam War. South Vietnam fought North Vietnam between 1957 and 1975.

*leeches:* bloodsucking worms

*spouses:* marriage partners; husbands or wives

*eligible:* unmarried

After the rice has been separated from the stalks and dried, the husks and dirt must be removed. This woman uses a bamboo tray to toss the rice into the air. The wind blows away the impurities.

home for further processing. The very best rice, of course, we gave back to Mother Earth. This seed rice was called *lua giong* and we put it into great jars which we filled with water. The wet rice was then packed under a haystack to keep warm. The nutrients, moisture, and heat helped the rice seeds to sprout, and after three days (during which we watered and fertilized the seedbed like a garden), we recovered the jars and cast the fertile *geo ma* seeds onto the ground we had prepared. But this was rice we would enjoy another day. The preparation of rice to eat now was our highest **priority**.

When the *lua chet* was dry, we stored a portion in the main part of our house, which we called *nha tren*, or top house, because my father slept there and it held our **ancestral shrine**. This rice was kept in bins behind a bamboo curtain which was also a hiding place for valuables, weapons and supplies, and little kids like me when soldiers came to the village. . . .

Once the brown rice grains were out of their shells, we shook them in wide baskets, tossing them slightly into the air so that the wind could carry off the husks. When finished, the rice was now ready to go inside where it became "floor rice" and was pounded in a bowl to crack the layer of bran that contained the sweet white kernel. When we swirled the cracked rice in a woven **colander**, the bran fell through the holes and was collected to feed the pigs. The broken rice that remained with the good kernels was called *tam* rice, and although it was fit to eat, it was not very good and we used it as chicken feed (when the harvest was good) or collected it and shared it with beggars when the harvest was bad.

We always blamed crop failures on ourselves—we had not worked hard enough or, if there was no other explanation, we had failed to adequately honor our ancestors. Our solution was to pray more and sacrifice more and eventually things always got better. Crops ruined by soldiers were another matter. We knew prayer was useless because soldiers were human beings, too, and the god of nature meant for them to work out their own **karma** just like us.

In any event, the journey from seedling to rice bowl was long and laborious and because each grain was a symbol of life, we never wasted any of it. Good rice was considered god's gemstone—*hot ngoc troi*—and was cared for accordingly on pain of divine punishment. Even today a peasant seeing lightning will crouch under the table and look for lost grains in order to escape the next bolt. And parents must never strike children, no matter how naughty they've been, while the child is eating rice, for that would interrupt the sacred **communion** between rice-eater and rice-maker. Like my brothers and sisters, I learned quickly the advantages of chewing my dinner slowly.

*karma:* fate; destiny

*communion:* sharing in which a blessing is bestowed

A mother has prepared a bowl of rice for her child. Rice, the main food in the Vietnamese diet, is sometimes mixed with a small portion of fish or vegetables.

About 75 percent of the Vietnamese people are farmers. Most live in villages in the two main rice-growing regions. These regions are the Red River delta in the north and the Mekong delta in the south. Improvements in rice technology have increased rice production. Village life and religious practices revolve around rice farming. Le Ly Hayslip fled her village in 1970 during the Vietnam War and came to the United States to live.

Excerpt from *When Heaven and Earth Changed Places* by Le Ly Hayslip, pp. 5–9.
Copyright © 1989 by Le Ly Hayslip and Charles Jay Wurts. Used by permission of Doubleday, a division of Bantam, Doubleday, Dell Publishing Group, Inc.

# THE PACIFIC REALM

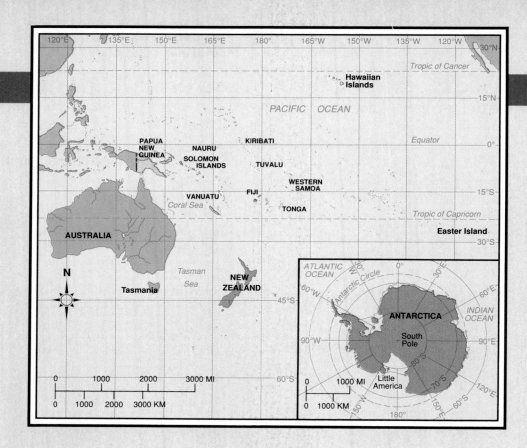

**koalas:** furry mammals that look like teddy bears

*Melanesia:* group of islands south of the equator in the western South Pacific Ocean. The name means "black islands," a reference to the dark-skinned people who live there.

*Micronesia:* group of islands north of the equator in the Western Pacific Ocean. The name means "small islands."

*Polynesia:* group of islands in the central and southeastern Pacific Ocean. The name means "many islands."

In and around the isolated southern Pacific Ocean lie Australia, Oceania, and Antarctica—three diverse and exotic places. A traveler to these three areas might encounter penguins, platypuses, or palm trees. In Australia, he would find some of the driest land in the world. In Antarctica, he would find the coldest land in the world. In Oceania, he would find, and probably walk along, some of the most beautiful beaches in the world.

Australia is a dry and dusty land. A rust-red or tawny dust covers much of the "land down under," the smallest and flattest continent in the world. Nonetheless, more than half of the land in Australia is good for grazing cattle and sheep. Kangaroos graze here too, and **koalas** chew eucalyptus leaves. In the driest area, the remote central "outback," the land is parched and empty, and the cycle of droughts and flash floods is maddening for those who live there.

Australia is a land of immigrants. The original inhabitants were the Aboriginals who have lived there for thousands of years. But not until about 200 years ago did Europeans, mostly from England, make a claim on the land. Today Australia's population is 16 million strong, and non-Europeans make up just one percent of the total. Most of the people live in sprawling urban centers, such as Sydney, Brisbane, and Canberra, on the green eastern coast where the most rain falls.

Plenty of rain falls on the many tiny islands of Oceania. So many islands make up Oceania—about 25,000 of them—that some have never been named. Geographers divide the islands into three main island groups: **Melanesia, Micronesia,** and **Polynesia.** Some of these islands were formed by volcanoes; others were slowly built up by **coral polyps,** one coral skeleton on top of another. The climate is hot and humid on most of these islands, but the landscapes vary. Some islands are nothing but sand; others are bursting with plant life. Some are flat, others mountainous. On one of these islands—grassy, windswept Easter Island in Polynesia—awesome statues stand guard. Carved from the volcanic stone called tuff, the statues present a mystery yet to be solved.

*coral polyps:* small sea creatures whose skeletons form coral reefs

Antarctica is almost twice the size of Australia. It is even drier, it is much colder, and it is practically uninhabited, a better home for penguins and seals than for humans. Antarctica is a world of ice surrounding the South Pole. Ice more than a mile thick covers the land. Ice on the water welds islands together and clogs bays. Icebergs, like small mountains, drift in the nearby sea.

Antarctic winds that howl over the landscape can reach 120 miles an hour. They lower the subzero temperatures of the land even further. But while the land is barren, life thrives in the frigid waters of Antarctica. Emperor penguins and Weddell seals raise their young here. And more than seven kinds of whales, including the humpback and the killer whale, find plenty to eat in these waters.

The interior of Australia is dotted with low-lying mountain ranges and vast stretches of sandy, dry land called the bush.

In this unit three people who have visited some of these distant places tell their stories.

- Traveler Bruce Chatwin goes to the heart of **Australia** and describes a startling walk through the bush.
- John Dos Passos shares his lifelong interest in the statues of **Easter Island** in Polynesia.
- Admiral Richard Byrd shares the sights and sounds he experienced when he returned to the continent of **Antarctica** on his second expedition in 1933.

# Australian Adventure

**" It was madness to go up on the mountain."**

**Bruce Chatwin**

Much of Australia's interior is covered with short grasses and scrub brush.

*Arkady:* man with whom Chatwin traveled

*caravan:* mobile home, trailer

*Mount Liebler:* mountain near the ranch where Chatwin was staying

*Rolf:* friend of Chatwin

*rucksack:* backpack

*game-drives:* herding animals

*pointillist:* style of painting using small dots

*spinifex:* an Australian grass

*Lawrence:* (D.H.) English novelist

*wallaby:* marsupial related to the kangaroo

**W**riter Bruce Chatwin set out to explore the untamed region of Australia known as "bush." Along the way he discovered many interesting people, places, and things. He viewed firsthand the lifestyle of the Aboriginals (Aborigines), the native people of Australia. During his travels, Chatwin kept a journal. In this excerpt he describes the plants and animals he saw during one of his adventures.

It was still cool and bright in the early morning.

"I thought I'd go for a walk today," I said.

We were expecting **Arkady** any day and, each morning, at work in the **caravan**, I promised myself a walk up **Mount Liebler**.

"Take water," said **Rolf**. "Take three times the water you think you need."

I pointed out the way I planned to climb.

"Don't worry," he said. "We've got trackers who'd find you in a couple of hours. But you *must* take the water."

I filled my water flask, put two extra bottles in my **rucksack,** and set out. On the edge of the settlement, I passed a lady's handbag hanging from a tree.

I walked over a plateau of sandhills and crumbly red rock, broken by gulches which were difficult to cross. The bushes had been burnt for **game-drives**, and bright green shoots were sprouting from the stumps.

I was climbing steadily, and, looking down at the plain, I understood why Aboriginals choose to paint their land in **"pointillist"** dots. The land *was* dotted. The white dots were **spinifex**; the blueish dots were eucalyptus, and the lemon-green dots were some other kind of tufty grass. I understood, too, better than ever, what **Lawrence** meant by the "peculiar, lost weary aloofness of Australia."

A **wallaby** got up and went bounding downhill. I then saw, on the far side of the chasm, something big in the shade of a tree. At first I

112

thought it might be a **Giant Red**, until I realised it was a man.

I **shinned up** the far side to find **Old Alex**, naked, his spears along the ground and his velvet coat wrapped in a bundle. I nodded and he nodded.

"Hello," I said. "What brings you here?"

He smiled, bashful at his nakedness, and barely opening his lips, said: "Footwalking all the time all over the world."

I left him to his **reverie** and walked on. The spinifex was thicker than ever. At times I despaired of finding a way through, but always, like **Ariadne's thread**, there *was* a way through.

I next fell for the temptation —the temptation of touching a **hedgehog**—to put my hand on a clump: only to find my palm was stuck with spines an inch or so before I'd expected. As I picked them out, I remembered something Arkady had said, "Everything's spiny in Australia. Even a **goanna**'s got a mouthful of spines."

I clambered up the **screes of the escarpment** and came out on a knife edge of rock. It really did look like the **perenty lizard**'s tail. Beyond, there was a tableland with some trees along a dried-up watercourse. The trees were leafless. They had rumpled grey bark and tiny scarlet flowers that fell to the ground like drops of blood.

I sat, exhausted, in the half-shade of one of these trees. It was **infernally** hot.

A short way off, two male **butcher birds**, black and white like magpies, were calling **antiphonally** across a ravine. One bird would lift his beak vertically and let out three long whooping notes, followed by three **ascending** shorts. The rival would then pick up the refrain, and repeat it.

"Simple as that," I said to myself. "Exchanging notes across a frontier."

I was lying spreadeagled against the tree-trunk with one leg dangling over the bank, swigging greedily from the water flask. I now knew what Rolf meant by **dehydration**. It was madness to go on up the mountain. I would have to go back the way I'd come.

The butcher birds were silent. Sweat poured over my eyelids so that everything seemed blurred and out of scale. I heard the clatter of loose stones along the bank, and looked up to see a monster approaching.

It was a giant **lace-monitor**, the lord of the mountain, Perenty himself. He must have been seven feet long. His skin was pale **ochre**, with darker brown markings. He licked the air with his lilac tongue. I froze. He clawed his way forward: there was no way of telling if he'd seen me. The claws passed within two inches

Australia has animals that are not found anywhere else in the world. These small kangaroos are called wallabies.

*Giant Red:* red kangaroo

*shinned up:* climbed

*Old Alex:* Aboriginal man who was an excellent hunter

*reverie:* daydreaming

*Ariadne's thread:* in Greek mythology, the thread that Ariadne gave to Theseus to help him escape from a maze

*hedgehog:* small mammal with spines on its back

*goanna:* any of several types of large lizards

*screes of the escarpment:* piles of loose stones at the foot of a steep slope

*perenty lizard:* large goanna

*infernally:* awfully

*butcher birds:* birds that kill their prey and then hang it on thorns

*antiphonally:* singing back and forth

*ascending:* rising in pitch

*dehydration:* dryness due to a lack of fluids

*lace-monitor:* the largest Australian goanna. Some grow to more than eight feet long and move as fast as a horse.

*ochre:* yellow or reddish-brown color

**113**

*benign:* harmless

*bestiary:* collection of fables about real and mythical animals

*initiation time:* time during which Aboriginal boys become full members of the tribe

*apparition:* ghostly figure

*Rainbow Snake:* frightening mythical creature

*yeti-like:* like the legendary Abominable Snowman

*marsupial lion:* meat-eating wolf-like animal of Australia; almost extinct

*megafauna:* animals that can be seen by the unaided eye in an area of land

of my boot. Then he turned full-circle and, with a sudden burst of speed, shot off the way he'd come.

The perenty has a nasty set of teeth, but is harmless to man unless cornered: in fact, apart from scorpions, snakes and spiders, Australia is exceptionally **benign**.

All the same the Aboriginals have inherited a **bestiary** of monsters and bugaboos: with which to menace their children, or torment young men at **initiation time.** I remembered Sir George Grey's description of the Boly-yas: a flap-eared **apparition,** more stealthily vengeful than any other creature, which would consume the flesh, but leave the bones. I remembered the **Rainbow Snake**.

And I remembered Arkady talking about the *Manu-manu*: a fanged, **yeti-like** creature which moved underground, prowled the camps at night, and made off with unwary strangers.

The first Australians, I reflected, will have known real monsters such as the *Thylacaleo,* or "**marsupial lion.**" There was also a perenty lizard thirty feet long. Yet there was nothing in the Australian **megafauna** to contend with the horrors of the African bush.

I fell to wondering whether the violent edge of Aboriginal life—the blood-vengeance and bloody initiations—might stem from the fact of their having no proper beasts to contend with.

The culture of the Aborigines is closely tied to nature. This Aboriginal painting on tree bark shows some of the birds and reptiles that roam the Australian outback.

The frilled dragon or lizard has a collar of skin around its neck that flares out when it is threatened by another animal. This action makes the lizard look much larger than it really is.

I dragged myself to my feet, climbed across the ridge, and looked down over **Cullen settlement.**

I thought I could see an easier way down, which would avoid having to cross the gulches. This "easy way" turned out to be a rock-slide, but I arrived at the bottom in one piece and walked home along a streambed.

There was a trickle of water in the stream, and bushes grew along it. I splashed some water over my face, and walked on. I had raised my right leg to take a step forward and heard myself saying, "I am about to tread on something that looks like a green pine-cone." What I had not yet seen was the head of the **king-brown**, about to strike, rearing up behind a bush. I put my legs into reverse and drew back, very slowly . . . one . . . two . . . one . . . two. The snake also withdrew, and slithered off into a hole. I said to myself, "You're being very calm"—until I felt the waves of nausea.

I got back to Cullen at half past one.

Rolf looked me up and down and said, "You look quite shattered, **mate**."

*Cullen settlement:* ranch where Chatwin stayed

*king-brown:* poisonous snake

*mate:* friend

Because the Australian bush is very dry and wild, it is not densely populated. The main occupations in the area are ranching and mining. Most ranches, or stations, as they are called in the bush, are used for raising sheep or cattle. The area's largest settlements are mining towns. The most untamed part of the bush is called the "outback." About 60 percent of the world's opals are mined in the outback.

# Mysterious Statues

The towering stone figures on Easter Island were carved from volcanic rock. Some are nearly 40 feet tall and weigh 50 tons.

" The enormous figure with its masklike face and longlobed ears loomed solitary above our heads."

**John Dos Passos**

*restored:* made to look as it did originally

*Tahai:* a region on the west coast of Easter Island

*monolith:* statue made of one large piece of stone

*solitary:* alone

*comparatively:* by comparison; fairly

*beetling:* jutting

*submerged:* underwater

*occupation:* settlement

*conventional:* common; usual

*immensity:* great size

*reckoned:* thought; figured

*quarry:* place where stones are cut

Easter Island is a small island located in the South Pacific Ocean. Three volcanoes formed Easter Island, giving it a triangular shape. Scientists believe the island was settled around A.D. 400. The island is most famous for the large stone statues carved by its early settlers. Made of stone found on the island, these statues are huge human figures. In 1969 John Dos Passos went to Easter Island to learn more about these strange statues. ∞

The most completely **restored** statue on Easter Island is at a place called **Tahai**. The restored **monolith** stands on a low headland, a piece of sculpture that takes a lot of looking at. . . .

The enormous figure with its masklike face and longlobed ears loomed **solitary** above our heads. . . .

Like all of them the figure faces inland. The evenly placed rounded stones of the paved court which it faced have been restored. . . . The local name for the platforms is *ahu* and for the statues *moai*. . . .

Everything about Easter Island is surprising. You arrive expecting the terrain to look very ancient but geologically at least the island is **comparatively** recent. The **beetling** hills themselves are new, geologically speaking. According to the geologists

the island was raised above the sea by volcanic action, bursting out of some fold of the great **submerged** mountain chain known as the East Pacific Ridge. The latest volcanic activity might have taken place as recently as a thousand and certainly not earlier than two or three thousand years ago. . . . This youthfulness of the land sets a limit to the period of human **occupation**. . . .

The statues . . . all follow a **conventional** design, but different stages of erosion and the variations of sun and shadow give them different expressions. . . .

Their sheer **immensity** is overwhelming. The largest standing on the slope measures more than thirty-seven feet and is **reckoned** to weigh sixty-four tons. An unfinished giant still attached to the **quarry** wall measures eighty-two feet. . . .

116

You have to examine some part of the surface which has been protected from the weather to appreciate the **high finish** the carvings originally had. Their present **roughhewn** look is the result of the erosion of the volcanic **tuff** they are carved out of by centuries of wind and rain. Some investigators think that, like the **Greek marbles**, they were originally painted.

The finest piece of work of them all, in fact in my opinion the finest thing on Easter Island, is the buried **basalt** monster . . . on the southern slope of **Rano Raraku**. The statue had been buried so deep that none of the islanders knew of its existence. It is thought to date from the early period before A.D. 1100. It represents a naked man squatting on his heels. The head, exaggerated in size, is tilted up as if looking into immense distances. The cheekbones are broad, the eyesockets deep. A small chinbeard gives the face an oddly **aristocratic** look. The quality of the carving is hardly **diminished** by the **pitting** and erosion of centuries. The people who produced this sculpture must have had long years of technical training behind them.

*high finish:* very smooth and polished surface

*roughhewn:* poorly finished; not smooth

*tuff:* rock formed from volcanic ash

*Greek marbles:* ancient Greek statues carved from marble

*basalt:* dark volcanic rock

*Rano Raraku:* extinct volcano on Easter Island. More than 100 statues have been found inside and outside the crater's wall.

*aristocratic:* upper class; proud

*diminished:* lessened

*pitting:* small holes on a surface

Easter Island is only 11 miles across at its widest point and about 15 miles in length. This crater was formed by one of the three volcanoes that created the island.

—————————— ∽ ——————————

Hundreds of statues have been found on Easter Island. There is much debate over where the carvers of the statues came from. Some scientists think that Peruvians first settled the island. Two facts support this idea. Peruvians of that time were skilled stoneworkers. So were the early Easter Islanders. Also, ocean currents that could have carried the settlers tend to move westward from Peru to Easter Island.

From John Dos Passos, *Easter Island* (New York: Doubleday, 1971), pp. 123–25, 134–35. Reprinted by permission.

# Return to Antarctica

" A crystal quiet lay over the place . . . and the surface was smooth as the slickest satinwood. "

**Richard E. Byrd**

Rear Admiral Richard E. Byrd was an aviator and explorer. Here he is shown in the cockpit of a plane that he flew to Antarctica.

*meteors:* bodies of matter from space that fall through Earth's atmosphere

*Barrier wall:* Great Ice Barrier; a flat wall of ice 150 to 200 feet above sea level

*ice foot:* narrow border of sea ice that is frozen to the shore

*bedlam:* confusion

*sledges:* sleds used to carry loads over ice and snow. They are usually pulled by dog teams.

*wrathful:* angry

*Ver-Sur-Mer Inlet:* strip of water that extends into land. It was named after a French village by Byrd's party.

*plumb:* straight up and down

*swales:* low areas of land

**R**ear Admiral Richard Byrd made his first journey to Antarctica in 1928. There he built Little America—a base on the Ross Ice Shelf. He also led the first flight over the South Pole. Byrd returned to Antarctica in 1933 and stayed until 1935. During this time he and the scientists with him studied **meteors**, weather, and Earth's magnetic pull. Here Byrd describes his return to Little America. ∞

Five hundred yards off the east **Barrier wall** Commodore Gjertsen stopped the ship. The motor sailer was lowered, and fifteen of us went aboard. About three miles north of Little America we made the landing, bringing the boat alongside a gentle incline of **ice foot**. We waited while the boat returned to the ship to pick up the dog teams. The moment the dogs set foot on the Barrier the Antarctic peace was gone. **Bedlam** shouted in. Once more on firm land, after three and one half months on a heaving steel deck, the huskies went utterly mad. They yipped, and they barked; they ate snow, and they rolled in it: they wriggled out of harnesses, and tore in wild circles around the landing place. In no time the place was a shambles of broken harnesses, overturned **sledges,** slithering huskies and exceedingly **wrathful** drivers.

Leaving the dog drivers to collect their teams, Haines, Petersen, Noville, and I started on foot for Little America. Sinking to the knee at every step we toiled up the slope. Now three black specks slowly lifted above the glistening ridge—the three radio towers! On the crest Little America was revealed—the shallow valley at the head of **Ver-Sur-Mer Inlet**, the tall steel towers one of which was leaning out of **plumb**, a cluster of low bamboo antennae poles, and strange, unremembered things that the snows of four winters hadn't covered. A crystal quiet lay over the place, over the smooth and rounded **swales** running to the horizon; not a snow crystal was out of place, and the surface was smooth as the slickest satinwood.

In a little while we stood over the Administration building. The snow had deepened three or four feet. The ventilators and the stove pipe were barely **awash**, but the cleated **anemometer** pole stood a good five feet above the surface; and curiously, a broom, stuck in by the handle, was there, an irrelevant suggestion of domestic **felicity**.

Bill Haines' face, as he took in these familiar things, was good to see. "Bet I could dig down and find my old **theodolite** stand," he said. "You're on," I said, "here's the shovel." Bill's face fell. He looked at the shovel with strong distaste. "Listen," he said. "Four years ago, when I put down one of those awful things, I took a pledge—a solemn pledge—that I'd cut off my right arm before I'd touch a snow shovel again. And [darned] if you don't put one in my hand the moment we land!" It may be a classic phrase that the smell of powder **exhilarates** old war-horses, but I've never seen a veteran explorer show anything but the deepest **melancholia** at the sight of a snow shovel.

By that time the dog teams had pulled up, bringing more recruits. Neither Haines nor I was exactly certain where to start digging. We paced off the distance from the stove pipe, trying to remember how many steps we used to take from the stove to the **vestibule** opening into the tunnels. However, after an argument, a large hole was started. Three or four feet down, Haines broke through a shell of hard blue ice, and uncovered the **tarpaulin** roofing the old balloon station. In short order he drove a hole through that, and disappeared. In a little while we heard him chuckling. We plunged in after him.

Fourteen feet down, at the bottom of the square balloon station, with its ledge for the theodolite tripod still intact, we turned left into the vestibule. Bill had left the door open. We could hear him stumbling around in the dark. A faint ghostly **fluorescence** illuminated the ice packed around the windows.

**awash:** above the surface of the snow

**anemometer:** gauge that measures wind speed

**felicity:** happiness

**theodolite:** surveying tool that measures horizontal and vertical angles

**exhilarates:** excites; makes lively

**melancholia:** sadness

**vestibule:** small room that serves as an entrance

**tarpaulin:** waterproof canvas

**fluorescence:** light

Research vessels explore the coasts of Antarctica in summer. Only large ice-breaking ships can make their way through the frozen waters surrounding Antarctica in the winter.

Petersen struck a match. By the light of it I found a fruit jar, half full of kerosene which, surprisingly, was still there. The wick burned, and as the glow strengthened the shadows fell back.

It wouldn't be right to say that the place looked as if we had left it only yesterday. The roof had sagged under the crushing weight of ice. Several of the main beams had cracked. They lay splintered across the top bunks. A film of ice lay over the walls, and from the ceiling hung thick clusters of ice crystals, which were brighter than jewels when the light caught them. The haste with which the building had been evacuated was everywhere in evidence. Torn parkas and windproofs, unmatched **mukluks**, dirty underwear and odds and ends of all sorts were scattered about. By the looks of it you would have thought a tornado had struck the place. I was a trifle ashamed that we had left that mess behind us, and glad we could do our own housecleaning.

On a table stood a coffee pot, a piece of roast beef with a fork stuck in it, and half a loaf of bread. Four years before, Dr. Coman had lunched off them while he waited for the last sledge to come back for Mason, who lay ill with appendicitis. It evoked queer memories to come upon that. There was a time, back in February 1930, when it looked as if Mason were too ill to be moved, and some of us might have to spend a second year. On the bunk walls were 1929 calendars, with the days scratched off. . . .

Meanwhile a second group dug down into the Mess Hall, breaking through the roof of McKinley's photographic laboratory. This building lay about two hundred yards west of the Administration Building. We hurried over to have a look. They told me that the door from the photo lab

to the main house was open when they got to the bottom. Well, that was another reality out of the past. McKinley was never known to close a door behind him. . . .

The Mess Hall, perhaps because of its **stauncher** construction, was in good shape. The roof was undamaged, in spite of the six feet of snow and ice that had accumulated on it. The shack needed a bit of tidying up, that was all. Cans of baked beans, meats, coffee, cocoa, and powdered milk were neatly racked behind the galley stove.

While we were standing there the telephone rang. I'm not joking; it actually rang. . . . Nobody moved for a second. . . . Petersen had found the telephone and pressed the buzzer. We heard him laugh. Poulter answered in the Ad Building. "By yimminy," said Pete, "she works!"

A set of boxing gloves hung from a nail overhead. There was a

Huge ice shelves make ideal runways for research planes. Some are several thousand feet thick.

*mukluks:* Eskimo boots made of sealskin, reindeer skin, canvas, or rubber

*stauncher:* sturdier; stronger

girl's picture on the wall. Strom's accordion, on which he used to play delightful Norwegian folk songs, was in his bunk. The phonograph was on the long mess table, and the needle was poised over a record. . . .

Then the most amazing thing of all happened. Petersen idly flipped a switch. The lights went on. Not brightly—just a dim, faint glow in the bulbs, but undeniably they burned.

On the stove were cooking pans full of frozen food. There was coal in the **scuttle.** A fire was made in the kitchen stove, the food was warmed, and found to be as good as the day we left, four years ago. The seal and whale meat and beef in the tunnel were perfectly preserved.

*scuttle:* bucket used to carry coal

Millions of penguins gather on the icy shores of Antarctica. They live in colonies called rookeries and build their nests on rocks or ice. Penguins use their wings to swim, but are unable to fly.

The United States is not the only country that has explored Antarctica. Argentina, Australia, Chile, France, Great Britain, New Zealand, and Norway have also explored the region. Unlike the United States, these countries have claimed parts of Antarctica as their own. Several other countries have set up research stations there. All of these countries have agreed to use the continent mainly for research. Scientists in Antarctica are studying gravity, earthquakes, the **icecap**, and the **ozone** layer.

*icecap:* ice layer more than a mile thick on the surface of Antarctica

*ozone:* layer of the atmosphere that protects Earth from harmful rays of the sun

From Richard E. Byrd, *Discovery* (New York: G.P. Putnam's Sons, 1935), pp. 71–73. Reprinted by permission of Richard E. Byrd III.

# INDEX

# *PHOTO CREDITS*